The Entrepreneurship Movement and the University

Other Palgrave Pivot titles

Emma Bell: **Soft Power and Freedom under the Coalition: State-Corporate Power and the Threat to Democracy**

Ben Ross Schneider: **Designing Industrial Policy in Latin America: Business-State Relations and the New Developmentalism**

Tamer Thabet: **Video Game Narrative and Criticism: Playing the Story**

Raphael Sassower: **Compromising the Ideals of Science**

David A. Savage and Benno Torgler: **The Times They Are A Changin': The Effect of Institutional Change on Cooperative Behaviour at 26,000 ft over Sixty Years**

Mike Finn (editor): **The Gove Legacy: Education in Britain after the Coalition**

Clive D. Field: **Britain's Last Religious Revival? Quantifying Belonging, Behaving, and Believing in the Long 1950s**

Richard Rose and Caryn Peiffer: **Paying Bribes for Public Services: A Global Guide to Grass-Roots Corruption**

Altug Yalcintas: **Creativity and Humour in Occupy Movements: Intellectual Disobedience in Turkey and Beyond**

Joanna Black, Juan Carlos Castro, and Ching-Chiu Lin: **Youth Practices in Digital Arts and New Media: Learning in Formal and Informal Settings**

Wouter Peeters, Andries De Smet, Lisa Diependaele and Sigrid Sterckx: **Climate Change and Individual Responsibility: Agency, Moral Disengagement and the Motivational Gap**

Mark Stelzner: **Economic Inequality and Policy Control in the United States**

Michelle Bayefsky and Bruce Jennings: **Regulating Preimplantation Genetic Diagnosis in the United States**

Eileen Piggot-Irvine: **Goal Pursuit in Education Using Focused Action Research**

Serenella Massidda: **Audiovisual Translation in the Digital Age: The Italian Fansubbing Phenomenon**

John Board, Alfonso Dufour, Yusuf Hartavi, Charles Sutcliffe and Stephen Wells: **Risk and Trading on London's Alternative Investment Market: The Stock Market for Smaller and Growing Companies**

Franklin G. Mixon, Jr: **Public Choice Economics and the Salem Witchcraft Hysteria**

Elisa Menicucci: **Fair Value Accounting: Key Issues Arising from the Financial Crisis**

DOI: 10.1057/9781137401014.0001

palgrave▶pivot

# The Entrepreneurship Movement and the University

Creso M. Sá
*Academic Director, Graduate Education, Ontario Institute for Studies in Education, University of Toronto, Canada*

and

Andrew J. Kretz
*PhD Student, Ontario Institute for Studies in Education, University of Toronto, Canada*

THE ENTREPRENEURSHIP MOVEMENT AND THE UNIVERSITY
Copyright © Creso M. Sá and Andrew J. Kretz, 2015.

All rights reserved.

First published in 2015 by
PALGRAVE MACMILLAN®
in the United States—a division of St. Martin's Press LLC,
175 Fifth Avenue, New York, NY 10010.

Where this book is distributed in the UK, Europe and the rest of the world, this is by Palgrave Macmillan, a division of Macmillan Publishers Limited, registered in England, company number 785998, of Houndmills, Basingstoke, Hampshire RG21 6XS.

Palgrave Macmillan is the global academic imprint of the above companies and has companies and representatives throughout the world.

Palgrave® and Macmillan® are registered trademarks in the United States, the United Kingdom, Europe and other countries.

ISBN: 978-1-137-40102-1  EPUB
ISBN: 978-1-137-40101-4  PDF
ISBN: 978-1-137-40265-3  Hardback

Library of Congress Cataloging-in-Publication Data is available from the Library of Congress.

A catalogue record of the book is available from the British Library.

First edition: 2015

www.palgrave.com/pivot

DOI: 10.1057/9781137401014

# Contents

| | |
|---|---|
| List of Figures | vi |
| List of Tables | vii |
| 1 The Entrepreneurship Movement | 1 |
| 2 Entrepreneurship in North America | 20 |
| 3 Public Policy for Entrepreneurship | 48 |
| 4 Entrepreneurship Learning on Campus | 77 |
| 5 Conclusions | 132 |
| Index | 149 |

# List of Figures

| | | |
|---|---|---|
| 2.1 | Entrepreneurial intentions in the United States | 22 |
| 2.2 | Nascent entrepreneurship rates in the United States and Canada | 23 |
| 2.3 | Entrepreneurship rates in the United States and Canada | 24 |
| 2.4 | The number of establishments in the United States born from new firms | 25 |
| 2.5 | The percent of new establishments in the United States born from new firms | 25 |
| 2.6 | The business entry rate in Canada | 26 |
| 2.7 | Survival rates of US establishments, by year started and number of years since starting | 27 |
| 2.8 | Employer establishment birth rates in the United States and Canada | 29 |
| 2.9 | Biopharmaceutical establishments by MSA, 2012 | 31 |
| 2.10 | US Information technology and analytical instruments established by MSA, 2012 | 32 |
| 2.11 | Entrepreneurs in the United States, by MSA, 2013 | 33 |
| 2.12 | Percent of entrepreneurs with a college or university education | 35 |
| 2.13 | Industries with entrepreneurs with a college or university education | 36 |
| 2.14 | University spin-off companies formed each year, 2001–2013 | 37 |
| 2.15 | Location of university spin-off companies formed during 2009–2013 | 39 |
| 2.16 | Canadian entrepreneurs with a college or university education | 40 |

# List of Tables

2.1  Metropolitan statistical areas with the largest share of college or university educated entrepreneurs, 2013 — 34
2.2  University spin-off companies created, by university from 2009 to 2013 — 38

palgrave▶pivot

www.palgrave.com/pivot

# 1
# The Entrepreneurship Movement

**Abstract:** *Entrepreneurship is widely accepted and even celebrated today in the United States and Canada. Since the 1980s, several economic, political, and social trends have thrust entrepreneurship into the public agenda and into higher education. This chapter provides an overview of how this "entrepreneurship movement" has been able to advance in higher education. In so doing, it frames the greater support for entrepreneurial learning and practice as not driven by financial or market incentives, but rather by pervasive economic, sociocultural and political trends unified in their enthusiasm and support for entrepreneurship. The entrepreneurship movement entails the ideation of entrepreneurship as an intrinsically positive set of ideas and values that can—or should—permeate higher education.*

Sá, Creso M. and Andrew J. Kretz. *The Entrepreneurship Movement and the University.* New York: Palgrave Macmillan, 2015. DOI: 10.1057/9781137401014.0004.

Entrepreneurship is widely embraced today in several sectors of society. In policy circles, there is great hope that promoting entrepreneurship is a solution for increasing employment and generating economic growth. Political leaders celebrate entrepreneurs for their creativity, talent, work ethic, resourcefulness, and risk-taking spirit.[1] Business writers, for their part, have spawned a whole genre of books on entrepreneurs and entrepreneurship, which is not confined to those interested in launching a new business; entrepreneurial ideas are applied to a range of issues, invariably framed as positive guidelines for thought and action.[2] Within popular culture, entrepreneurs are framed as contemporary heroes. One of 2010's most successful movies was *The Social Network*, a story of Mark Zuckerberg's creation of Facebook.[3] The film's plot would be unconceivable a few decades ago: a college student who devises a social network website out of his dorm room goes on to build one of the largest internet companies in the world. The success of this movie illustrates not only the cultural cache of entrepreneurs, but also the now commonly expected role of universities as sources of entrepreneurial talent and valuable high technology companies.

Indeed, today universities are expected to impart entrepreneurial skills to students, to support the formation of start-up companies, and to work productively with entrepreneurs to commercialize technologies. Moreover, initiatives to create an entrepreneurial mindset among students who may not be interested in launching businesses find support inside and outside higher education. This represents a significant change in the overall sentiment about entrepreneurship. Notwithstanding a few exceptions, the presence of entrepreneurial behaviors within the academy has traditionally been perceived as an intrusion into the scholarly and educational mission of higher education.[4] Scholars have generally had serious misgivings about commercial undertakings,[5] and higher education observers routinely cautioned against market-oriented and entrepreneurial values within universities and colleges.[6] However, the unease that prevailed in the past about the commingling of entrepreneurial and academic activities seems now slightly passé. University spin-offs are commonly portrayed as the prized outcomes of public investments in higher education, and many institutions publicize their efforts at teaching entrepreneurial skills to students. While these changes underscore broad support for entrepreneurial education, some academics remain uncertain about the place of entrepreneurship in the academy,[7] and not all are convinced that entrepreneurship can even be taught.[8] Nonetheless, the diffusion of entrepreneurship across colleges and universities represents a growing trend in the United States and Canada,[9] which has induced changes in educational expectations and practices in higher education.[10] Recognizing the significance of these changes, this book examines how this "entrepreneurship movement" has advanced in institutions of higher education in North America.

## The idea of entrepreneurship

Popular conceptions of the entrepreneur tend to follow the iconic image presented by early 20th-century economist Joseph Schumpeter. In Schumpeter's characterization, entrepreneurs are the agents who create and implement innovations such as new business models, products, and services that lead to "creative destruction," a process of economic renewal.[11] Schumpeter's work is now as commonly referenced in newspapers and popular magazines as it is in academic journals.[12] That the ideas of an early 20th-century Austrian economist have become mainstream is, in part, testimony to the pervasiveness of the idea of entrepreneurship today.

The Ewing Marion Kauffman Foundation, one of the largest supporters of entrepreneurship in the United States, captured the prevailing expectations for entrepreneurship in a 2009 report by the Kauffman Panel on Entrepreneurship Curriculum in Higher Education:

> Though entrepreneurship can involve—and thus often is mistaken for—invention, creativity, management, starting a small business, or becoming self-employed, it is neither identical with nor reducible to any of them. The defining trait of entrepreneurship is the creation of a novel enterprise that the market is willing to adopt.[13]

Yet, numerous authors have criticized the use of the term entrepreneurship to refer exclusively to firm start-up and business ownership.[14] Some propose that entrepreneurship is about discovering, evaluating, and exploiting opportunities, rather than solely creating a new company.[15] This broader focus has gained traction in several fields where the concept of entrepreneurship is applied to practically any active individual or group in any social context. Employees in existing firms can be "intrapreneurs;" administrators, politicians, or government officials can be "policy entrepreneurs;" artists can be "arts entrepreneurs;" and those involved in not-for-profit organizations can be "social entrepreneurs."[16] This diffusion of the concept arguably rests on the positive connotations of the idea of entrepreneurship as representing innovation, creativity, self-reliance, and positive-change-making.

This multidisciplinary framing and assimilation of entrepreneurship is directly related to its dissemination across universities and colleges. For instance, writing from a liberal arts perspective, Gatewood and West suggest that an entrepreneur is one "who takes advantage of knowledge and resources to identify and pursue opportunities that initiate change and create value in one's life and those of others."[17] By identifying entrepreneurship with proactive, opportunistic behavior that can generate meaningful change, scholars and practitioners across academic disciplines and professions are more commonly able to relate to the entrepreneurship movement.

## Trends driving the entrepreneurship movement

The now universal acclaim entrepreneurship receives for its role in spurring innovation, employment, and economic growth is a relatively new phenomenon. Since the 1980s, several economic, political, and social trends have thrust entrepreneurship into the public agenda and into higher education.[18]

The first trend relates to the place of entrepreneurs in an increasingly global, knowledge-based economy. Entrepreneurship is now central to current economic development theory,[19] which holds that the continued advance of globalization has shifted the comparative advantage of regions toward knowledge-based economic activity.[20] The notion of the global knowledge economy implies that traditional sources of competitiveness, such as low labor costs and favorable tax regimes, have become easily eroded by globalization. As a result, the only durable source of comparative advantage is the ability of firms to continually innovate through new products, services, distribution channels, and business models. Considering their role in bringing new innovations to market, start-ups have become important in this context, making entrepreneurs (particularly highly educated entrepreneurs) central to the mobilization and diffusion of new ideas and technologies. Moreover, large corporations in several industries have increasingly turned to external sources of innovation, including start-up companies and universities, as they seek to be more competitive and retain "leaner" research and development (R&D) laboratories.[21] Furthermore, in certain industries, such as biotechnology and information and communication technology (ICT), innovations have disproportionally come from start-up companies, often drawing on academic science.[22]

The second trend concerns shifts in public policy. Until the late 1980s, the prevailing wisdom was that large firms were responsible for employment growth and technological breakthroughs.[23] Large corporations, such as AT&T in the United States and Bell Canada/Northern Electric in Canada, employed tens of thousands of people and were the primary drivers of technological development. Small- and medium-sized enterprises were generally perceived as too small, vulnerable, and inefficient to successfully compete with larger, more established companies.[24] Large corporations were thus the beneficiaries of public policies for economic growth, in which policies sought to improve their efficiency and productivity.[25] These perceptions started to change following research findings in the early 1980s demonstrating that small firms generated the majority of new jobs in the US economy.[26] At the same time, accelerating globalization meant that large corporations were increasingly operating in large global decentralized chains of production, which underpinned the trends of offshoring and outsourcing. These trends disconnected the economic success of large companies from the generation of jobs in their home countries. The recognition of this scenario among policymakers prompted increased assistance to small firms. Unlike large corporations, small firms typically retain their operations domestically. By the second half of the 1990s, the relationship among firm creation, innovation, and economic growth became firmly established in policy discussions.[27]

Encouraging entrepreneurship—and not simply helping existing small businesses survive—has since then become an increasingly popular policy solution as a means to address the wicked problems of unemployment, economic dislocations, and lagging technological innovation.[28] Indeed, entrepreneurship policy emerged as a distinctive domain at various levels of government. Policymakers harbor expectations that promoting entrepreneurship will have a dramatic effect on economic revitalization and job creation.[29] In a global economy where capital and jobs are highly mobile, nurturing entrepreneurs provides policymakers with an opportunity to support—and to claim credit as being supporting—regional and local development.[30] Most regional and local policymakers now sponsor initiatives that promote entrepreneurship in targeted sectors; help commercialize research through start-ups; increase access to finance by launching or contributing to venture capital funds; provide tax incentives; and support incubators.[31] Because these initiatives often seek to accelerate the exploitation of research and innovations they tend to be linked to universities and colleges.

A third trend is the lowering of barriers to the establishment of new companies. New methods and technologies have reduced the costs of developing a customer base and shortened product development. ICT has enabled entrepreneurs to design new kinds of products and services with lower resource requirements.[32] In a globalized, ICT-linked economy, start-ups can leapfrog the lengthy business development process of earlier decades. Companies based in one country have near instantaneous contact with facilities in other countries, for instance to send specifications for a product's design. Moreover, new do-it-yourself tools such as 3D prints, and the emergence of makerspaces, have shortened the time and costs of designing new products and developing prototypes.[33] In addition, more forms of fundraising are also available to support start-ups. Venture capital used to be centered on such traditional hubs of entrepreneurship as Silicon Valley and Boston, where traditional venture capital funds were the chief agents. Today, with the participation of governments and universities, a larger number of organizations have entered this domain: super angel funds, university-based seed and venture capital, accelerators, and crowdsourcing are some alternatives to the big VC firms.[34] Altogether, lowered barriers for venture creation have also made it easier for universities to support entrepreneurs.

A fourth trend concerns the mobilization of interest groups around entrepreneurship in higher education. This is represented by a number of nongovernment organizations that actively promote the values of entrepreneurship, disseminate best practices, network across the sector, and provide support for programs. The Global Consortium of Entrepreneurship Centers (GCEC), for example, has multiple roles in promoting entrepreneurship. It hosts an annual conference, an awards program, and is home to the 21st Century Entrepreneurship Research Fellows.[35] VentureWell, formerly known as the National Collegiate Inventors and Innovators Alliance, is another major national organization that supports university faculty and students through multiple programs. Among them, faculty can obtain funding to develop courses and programs in technology-based entrepreneurship, and students can become "Innovation Fellows," receiving training on how to build entrepreneurship offerings on their campuses.[36] VentureWell also runs business idea competitions, provides seed funding to student entrepreneurs, and runs programs to instill entrepreneurial content and practice into university curricular and extracurricular offerings. In Canada, the Next36 is a private initiative whose goal is to address the country's "deficit of high impact entrepreneurs and nation-building business leaders."[37] It selects 36 postsecondary students from across the country for a nine-month program at the University of Toronto, in which they receive mentorship, seed capital, and formal instruction. The program culminates in a Venture Day where students showcase their mobile applications. Startup Canada also emerged recently to coalesce stakeholders in the entrepreneurship community, organizing events, awards, and other activities.[38] Foundations have also promoted the curricular integration of entrepreneurship into general undergraduate education, quite prominently in the case of the Kauffman Foundation, which has helped support the creation of new interdisciplinary entrepreneurship education programs at American universities.[39] The Coleman Foundation's Faculty Entrepreneurship Fellows Program also contributes to the diffusion of entrepreneurship across higher education institutions by sponsoring faculty who teach the subject in disciplines outside the school of business.[40]

The mobilization around entrepreneurship in higher education is also exemplified by support from successful entrepreneurs and private foundations to universities. Surveys of university entrepreneurship centers have found that approximately 44 percent of university entrepreneurship centers were named after private donors, and that roughly 43 percent of operating budges come from endowments and donations.[41] Benefactors have also for many years funded endowed positions in entrepreneurship in universities.[42] The Coleman Foundation is one benefactor of endowed positions in entrepreneurship, having established Coleman Chairs and Professorships in Entrepreneurship at ten colleges and universities in the United States. In Canada, private donors are also critical to entrepreneurship program budgets in universities. The John Dobson Foundation, for instance, promotes entrepreneurial activities and education, supporting entrepreneurship at 16 Canadian universities.[43]

The fifth trend is the sociocultural support for entrepreneurship. The entrepreneur resonates with prevailing cultural values and has captured the public's imagination. Entrepreneurs are now folk heroes, becoming subjects of films [i.e., *The Social Network* (2010) and *Jobs* (2013)] and featured in documentary television [*The New Heroes* (2005)]. Periodicals such as *Entrepreneur Magazine*, *Inc. Magazine*, *YFS* (Young, Fabulous & Self-Employed) *Magazine*, celebrate entrepreneurs and entrepreneurship, while popular television shows such as America's *Shark Tank* and its Canadian counterpart, *Dragon's Den*, showcase budding entrepreneurs as they seek funding from a panel of investors, themselves billed as entrepreneurs. A small wave of TV shows, such as HBO's comedy, *Silicon Valley*; Amazon's *Betas*; Bravo's 2012 reality series *Start-Ups: Silicon Valley* have joined-in. Toymaker Mattel has even released an Entrepreneur Barbie.[44] All these examples illustrate the cultural cache of entrepreneurs today. Moreover, this popularity is consistent with the views of Canadians and Americans about entrepreneurship. Almost two-thirds of Canadians believe that entrepreneurship is a good career choice, and nearly 60 percent believe that good entrepreneurship opportunities exist. Moreover, about 50 percent believe that they have the skills and knowledge to become entrepreneurs.[45] Approximately 47 percent of Americans believe that there are good opportunities for starting a business, and 56 percent believe that they have the capabilities to launch a business.[46]

Considering the enthusiasm for entrepreneurship, it is not surprising that interest in learning how to become an entrepreneur has increased among college students.[47] Although gauging the attitudes of students regarding entrepreneurship poses certain methodological challenges, research does provide useful insight. Survey data show that since 1993 the percent of incoming American university and college students who have chosen "business owner or proprietor" as their preferred career has generally increased. From 2008 to 2012, an average of 3 percent of incoming students chose business ownership as their preferred career. Small as this percentage may seem, about 43 percent of incoming freshmen reported that becoming successful in a business of their own was essential or very important.[48] A 2010 study reported that 40 percent of 18–21-year olds responded "yes" to the question: "Do you want to start your own business someday?" Twenty-five percent of respondents also agreed that "starting a business is much more desirable than other careers I might have;" and 16 percent agreed that "starting a non-profit venture is much more desirable than other careers I might have."[49] Stanford University's recent eclipse of Harvard University as prospective students' "number one dream school" in the Princeton Review has been linked to the former's reputation as an institution that develops student entrepreneurship.[50] MIT, historically the pioneer in such matters, similarly enjoys an enviable position as a hotbed of entrepreneurship in higher education. While few institutions can aspire to the status of Stanford or MIT, university and college entrepreneurship programs are celebrated in rankings such as those published by the *U.S. News and World Report, Entrepreneur Magazine, Success Magazine, Financial Times,* and *Bloomberg Businessweek.*

Finally, the idea of the "entrepreneurial university" has become ingrained over the last generation.[51] Although scientific research has long been important for technological development, and one can find early examples of academic entrepreneurship, the role of universities in relation to industry was reconfigured in the last quarter of the 20th century. The rise of science-based technologies such as biotech, ICT, and nanotechnology brought university research to the forefront in the quest for innovation. More generally, university research is an important input into industrial R&D activity, and occasionally generates new discoveries that are commercialized through new companies.[52] As such, they bring together multiple ingredients that are key inputs into knowledge-intensive entrepreneurial activity. To spur such activity, policymakers have urged universities to partner with industry to promote innovation, and facilitating such linkages has become an increasingly common strategy or aspiration among university leaders. This has involved a rationalization of technology transfer activity within universities, articulated as part of an economic development mission. Multiple organizational structures, programs, and administrative positions now exist to manage entrepreneurial activities. As universities now commonly emphasize engagement with the marketplace, proponents of entrepreneurship education have found amenable, or even eager, partners.

## The entrepreneurship movement and the university

This book builds upon previous work that has investigated the entrepreneurial university, but has a distinct focus. From the perspective of academic entrepreneurship, creating spin-off companies is one among many avenues for the commercialization of research and the promotion of innovation. "Entrepreneurship" in this context concerns the involvement of academics in spin-off activity as well as the patenting and licensing of inventions. Research in this area mainly adopts an economic perspective in investigating the determinants of firm formation, how spin-off activity can be maximized, their economic contributions, and their role in producing technological innovation.[53] Other researchers have viewed university entrepreneurship through the lens of "academic capitalism," which employs a sociological perspective to critique the engagement with higher education institutions in the commercial realm, highlighting shifts in the political economy and organizational responses that drive such activity.[54] It examines, for instance, how faculty and student involvement with companies can undermine academic orientations and values. Each of these bodies of work places the main focus away from the entrepreneurship movement as articulated here. For those investigating academic entrepreneurship, the focus lies on the university contribution to industrial innovation. In the scholarship on academic capitalism, the focus is on the regime of exchange under which higher education institutions operate.

This book sees the entrepreneurship movement as comprehending the advocacy, support, and implementation of ideas related to entrepreneurship to a growing range of areas and activities in higher education. The movement is neither restricted to the commercialization of research through spin-off companies, nor single-handedly focused on commercial outcomes. At its core is the diffusion of the idea of the entrepreneur, and of entrepreneurial thinking and behavior, to increasingly diverse areas of academic study and campus life. Overall, commitments to entrepreneurial thinking and practice span the research, education, and service missions of higher education. Thus, in contrast to prior conceptualizations of academic entrepreneurship,[55] this book sees greater support for entrepreneurial learning and practice as not driven entirely by financial or market incentives. Rather, it is the result of a pervasive economic, sociocultural, and political trends sketched out in this chapter.

To be sure, the entrepreneurship movement intersects with the ideation of the entrepreneurial university and an economic development mandate in higher education, but at the same time it follows its own logic. This logic is anchored in the entrepreneurship field, a shared sociostructural context consisting of practices and interests recognized and rewarded by a broad community of actors.[56] This community includes non-profit organizations evangelizing the virtues of entrepreneurship, philanthropists dedicated to supporting entrepreneurship, proponent of business models of entrepreneurship, public agencies providing services to entrepreneurs, and agents involved in supporting, capitalizing, and transacting with start-up companies. Inside universities, entrepreneurship education has emerged as an academic field of studies apart from the traditional business school curriculum. Although entrepreneurship courses and programs are typically found within business schools, the orientation and outcomes of entrepreneurship education are different than those provided by management education.[57] As entrepreneurial learning and practice take hold in universities, multiple participants in the field are drawn to campus and a range of academic actors participate in the field, including university faculty and administrators, alumni, donors, and students. This community vigorously promotes entrepreneurship as an intrinsically positive set of ideas and values that can—or should—permeate myriad aspects of economic and social life.

This book analyzes how entrepreneurship movement impacts higher education in Canada and the United States. Universities and colleges in these two countries have long histories of entrepreneurship education on campus and are leaders in promoting entrepreneurial endeavors. Many of the largest entrepreneurship ecosystems in the world are located in the United States and Canada. As discussed in Chapter 2, both countries are consistently ranked as leaders on most entrepreneurship indicators. The chapter examines the scope of entrepreneurship in the US and Canadian economies, as a way to position expectations about start-ups and higher education in a broader context.

Contemporary policy efforts to foster entrepreneurship with a focus on initiatives involving universities and high-technology ventures are analyzed in Chapter 3. Public policies for entrepreneurship are an important source of funding and coordination and of entrepreneurship at universities, and help to encourage and legitimize entrepreneurial activity and learning at universities.

Chapter 4 investigates the efforts being undertaken by universities and colleges to teach entrepreneurship and impart entrepreneurial attitudes and values in students. This chapter charts the development of entrepreneurship education and examines its diffusion from business schools to its becoming a university-wide phenomenon. It discusses how universities and colleges are increasingly supporting student entrepreneurs with a range of extracurricular programming, such as innovative incubation programs, start-up workshops, and venture seed funds.

The fifth and final chapter discusses the state and likely directions of the entrepreneurship movement. The chapter reflects on the institutional basis of the entrepreneurship movement in higher education, the agents actively promoting it, and concludes by discussing reasons why this movement is likely to remain relevant in the near future.

## Notes

1. Stephen Harper, *Statement by the Prime Minister of Canada on Global Entrepreneurship Week*, November 17, 2014, accessed December 11, 2014, http://pm.gc.ca/eng/news/2014/11/17/statement-prime-minister-canada-global-entrepreneurship-week; Barack Obama, *Presidential Proclamation— National Entrepreneurship Month, 2012*, November 1, 2012, accessed October 4, 2013, http://www.whitehouse.gov/the-press-office/2012/11/01/presidential-proclamation-national-entrepreneurship-month-2012.
2. For instance, David Bornstein, *How to Change the World: Social Entrepreneurs and the Power of New Ideas* (Oxford: Oxford University Press, 2007).
3. For awards and accolades, see "The Social Network (2010)," *The New York Times*, accessed December 20, 2014, http://www.nytimes.com/movies/movie/455955/The-Social-Network/awards.
4. MIT was the pioneer in welcoming entrepreneurial activity: see Roger L. Geiger, *To Advance Knowledge: The Growth of American Research Universities, 1900–1940* (Oxford: Oxford University Press, 2004); Henry Etkowitz, *MIT and the Rise of Entrepreneurial Science* (London: Routledge, 2002). In Canada, a tradition of entrepreneurial engagements developed at the University of Toronto, but they were viewed with suspicion until the late 1970s: Creso Sá, Andrew Kretz and Kristjan Sigurdson, "Techno-Nationalism and the Construction of University Technology Transfer," *Minerva* 51, no. 4 (2013): 443–464.
5. Charles Weiner, "Patenting and Academic Research: Historical Case Studies," *Science, Technology, and Human Values* (1987): 50–62; Rima D. Apple, "Patenting University Research: Harry Steenbock and the Wisconsin Alumni Research Foundation," *Isis* 80, no. 303 (1989): 375–394; Elliot A. Fishman, "MIT Patent Policy 1932–1946: Historical Precedents in University-Industry Technology Transfer" (PhD diss., University of Pennsylvania, Philadelphia, PA, 1996); Maryann P. Feldman and Pierre Desrochers, "Truth for Its Own Sake: Academic Culture and Technology Transfer at Johns Hopkins University," *Minerva* 42, no. 2 (2004): 105–126; Ali J. Ahmad and Sarah Ingle, "Relationships Matter: Case Study of a University Campus Incubator," *International Journal of Entrepreneurial Behaviour & Research* 17, no. 6 (2011): 626–644.
6. Sheila Slaughter, Teresa Campbell, Margaret Holleman, and Edward Morgan, "The 'Traffic' in Graduate Students: Graduate Students As Tokens of Exchange between Academe and Industry," *Science, Technology & Human*

Values 27, no. 2 (2002): 282–312; David L. Kirp, *Shakespeare, Einstein, and the Bottom Line: The Marketing of Higher Education* (Cambridge, MA: Harvard University Press, 2003); Derek C. Bok, *Universities in the Marketplace: The Commercialization of Higher Education* (Princeton, NJ: Princeton University Press, 2003); Peter D. Eckel, "Capitalizing on the Curriculum: The Challenge of Curricular Joint," *American Behavioral Scientist* 46, no. 7 (2003): 865–882; Jennifer Washburn, *University, Inc.: The Corporate Corruption of Higher Education* (New York: Basic Books, 2006).

7   Harvey A. Goldstein, "To What Extent Is Academic Entrepreneurship Taken for Granted Within Research Universities?" *Higher Education Policy* 23, no. 1 (2010): 1–15.

8   Karl H. Vesper and W. Ed McMullan, "Entrepreneurship: Today Courses, Tomorrow Degrees?" *Entrepreneurship Theory and Policy* 13, no. 1 (1988): 7–13; Colette Henry, Frances Hill, and Claire Leitch, "Entrepreneurship Education and Training: Can Entrepreneurship Be Taught? Part II," *Education + Training* 47, no. 3 (2005): 158–169; Peter G. Klein and J. Bruce Bullock, "Can Entrepreneurship Be Taught?" *Journal of Agricultural and Applied Economics* 38, no. 2 (2006): 429–439.

9   Deborah H. Streeter and John P. Jaquette Jr, "University-wide Entrepreneurship Education: Alternative Models and Current Trend," *The Southern Rural Sociological Association* 20, no. 2 (2004): 44–71; Jerome Katz, *2004 Survey of Endowed Positions in Entrepreneurship and Related Fields in the United States* (Kansas City, MO: Ewing Marion Kauffman Foundation, 2004); Teresa V. Menzies, *Entrepreneurship and the Canadian Universities: Strategies and Best Practices of Entrepreneurship Centres* (St. Catherines, Ontario: Faculty of Business, Brock University, 2009).

10  Elizabeth Hagan, *Entrepreneurship Education: A New Frontier for American Community Colleges* (PhD diss., Union Institute and University, 2004); G. Page West, Elizabeth J. Gatewood, and Kelly G. Shaver, *Handbook of University-wide Entrepreneurship Education* (Cheltenham, UK: Edward Elgar Publishing, 2009); Matthew M. Mars and Gary Rhoades, "Socially Oriented Student Entrepreneurship: A Study of Student Change Agency in the Academic Capitalism Context," *The Journal of Higher Education* 83, no. 3 (2012): 435–459; Kauffman Foundation, *Entrepreneurship Education Comes of Age on Campus* (Kansas City, MO: Ewing Marion Kauffman Foundation, 2013). Michael H. Morris, Donald F. Kuratko and Jeffrey R. Cornwall, *Entrepreneurship Programs and the Modern University* (Northampton, MA: Edward Elgar Publishing, 2013); Creso Sá, Andrew Kretz and Kristjan Sigurdson, *The State of Entrepreneurship Education in Ontario's Colleges and Universities* (Ontario: Higher Education Quality Council of Ontario, 2014).

11  Joseph A. Schumpeter, *The Theory of Economic Development* (London: Oxford University Press, 1934).

12  For example: Sharon Reier, "Half a Century Later, Economist's 'Creative Destruction' Theory Is Apt For the Internet Age: Schumpeter: The Prophet of Bust and Boom," *The New York Times*, June 10, 2000, http://www.nytimes.com/2000/06/10/your-money/10iht-mschump.t.html; Frank Rose, "The Father of Creative Destruction: Why Joseph Schumpeter Is Suddenly All the Rate in Washington," *Wired*, March 2002, accessed November 1, 2014, http://archive.wired.com/wired/archive/10.03/schumpeter.html; Gordon Pitts, "Fifty Years on, Schumpeter's Brand of Capitalism Is All the Rage," *Globe and Mail*, July 3, 2007, accessed November 1, 2014, http://www.theglobeandmail.com/report-on-business/fifty-years-on-schumpeters-brand-of-capitalism-is-all-the-rage/article724040/.
13  Kauffman Foundation, *A Report from the Kauffman Panel on Entrepreneurship Curriculum in Higher Education* (Kansas City, MO: Ewing Marion Kauffman Foundation, 2009), 5.
14  Brian McKenzie, Steve D. Ugbah, and Norman Smothers, "'Who Is An Entrepreneur?' Is It Still the Wrong Question?" *Academy of Entrepreneurship Journal* 13, no. 1 (2007); Morris, Kuratko, and Cornwall, *Entrepreneurship Programs and the Modern University*; Donald F. Kuratko, *Entrepreneurship: Theory, Process, Practice* (Mason, OH: South-western, 2014).
15  Scott Shane and S. Venkataraman, "The Promise of Entrepreneurship As a Field of Research", *The Academy of Management Review* 25, no. 1 (2000): 217–226.
16  David E. Pozen, "We Are All Entrepreneurs Now," *Wake Forest Law Review* 43 (2008): 283.
17  Elizabeth J. Gatewood and G. P. West III, "Responding to Opportunity and Need," *Peer Review* 7, no. 3 (2005): 12–14.
18  Scott Shane, *Academic Entrepreneurship: University Spinoffs and Wealth Creation* (Cheltenham, UK: Edward Elgar Publishing, 2004). Although university role in technology transfer and spin-offs have undoubtedly contributed to institutional capacity and acceptance of entrepreneurship, the drivers of the entrepreneurship trend differ from those attributed to faculty start-ups. Whereas science-based technologies, changes in patent laws, capital systems, university equity/TTO policies helped drive university-based spin-offs, entrepreneurship is driven by a changing economy, policy interest, lower barriers to business entry, and public interest.
19  David B. Audretsch, Isabel Grilo, and A Roy Thurik, "Explaining Entrepreneurship and the Role of Policy: A Framework," in *The Handbook of Research on Entrepreneurship Policy*, eds. David B. Audretsch, Isabel Grilo, and A. Roy Thurik (Cheltenham, UK: Edward Elgar Publishing, 2007), 1–17; Zoltan J. Acs, David B. Audretsch, and Robert J. Strom, eds., *Entrepreneurship, Growth, and Public Policy* (Oxford: Cambridge University Press, 2013).

20  David B. Audretsch and A. Roy Thurik, "What Is New About the New Economy: Sources of Growth in the Managed and Entrepreneurial Economies," *Industrial and Corporate Change*, 19 (2001): 795–821.
21  Henry Chesbrough, *Open Innovation: Researching a New Paradigm* (Oxford: Oxford University Press, 2003).
22  Roger L. Geiger and Creso Sá, *Tapping the Riches of Science: Universities and the Promise of Economic Growth* (Cambridge, MA: Harvard University Press: 2008).
23  John K. Galbraith, *American Capitalism: the Concept of Countervailing Power* (Boston, MA: Houghton Mifflin Co., 1952); Alfred D. Chandler, *Scale and Scope: The Dynamics of Industrial Capitalism* (Cambridge, MA: Harvard University Press, 1990); Magnus Henerkson and Jesper Roin, "Promoting Entrepreneurship In the Welfare State," in *The Handbook of Research on Entrepreneurship Policy*, eds. David B. Audretsch, Isabell Grilo, and A. Roy Thurik (Cheltenham, UK: Edward Elgar Publishing, 2007), 64–93.
24  Leondard W. Weiss, "Optimal Plant Scale and the Extent of Suboptimal Capacity," in *Essays on Industrial Organization in Honor of Joe S. Bain*, eds. Robert T. Masson and P. David Qualls (Cambridge, MA: Ballinger, 1964), 126–134; Clifford F. Pratten, *Economies of Scale In Manufacturing Industry* (Cambridge, MA: Cambridge University Press, 1971); Fredric M. Scherer, "Changing perspectives on the Firm Size Problem," in *Innovation and Technological Change: an International Comparison*, eds. Zoltán J. Acs and David B. Audretsch (Ann Arbor, MI: University of Michigan Press, 1991): 24–38.
25  David Audrescht, "The Emergence of the Entrepreneurial Society," *The Economic and Social Review* 40, No. 3 (2009): 255–268.
26  Lois Stevenson and Anders Lundström, "Dressing the Emperor: The Fabric of Entrepreneurship Policy," in *Handbook of Research on Entrepreneurship Policy*, eds. David B. Andretsch, Isabell Grilo, and A. Roy Thurik (Cheltenham, UK: Edward Elgar Publishing, 2007), 95.
27  Paul D. Reynolds, Michael Hay, and S. Michael Camp, *Global Entrepreneurship Monitor: 1999 Executive Report* (Babson College, London Business School and the Kauffman Center for entrepreneurial leadership), http://www.gemconsortium.org/docs/download/221.
28  OECD, *Thematic Overview of Entrepreneurship and Job Creation Policies* (Paris: OECD, 1995); OECD, *Small Businesses, Job Creation and Growth: Facts, Obstacles, and Best Practices* (Paris: OECD, 1997); OECD, *Fostering Entrepreneurship* (Paris: OECD, 1998); Jay Kayne, *State Entrepreneurship Policies and Programs* (Kansas City, MO: Kauffman Center for Entrepreneurial Leadership, 1999); Zoltán J. Acs and David B. Audretsch, *Innovation and Small Firms* (Cambridge, MA: MIT Press, 1990). In 1979, David Birch first provided evidence that small businesses were becoming the

primary engines of job growth in the United States. See David L. Birch, *The Job Generation Process* (an unpublished report prepared by the MIT Program on Neighborhood and Regional Change for the Economic Development Administration) (Washington DC: US Department of Commerce, 1979). David Halabisky, Policy Brief on Youth Entrepreneurship: Entrepreneurial Activities in Europe (OECD/European Union, 2012), accessed January 7, 2014, http://www.oecd.org/cfe/leed/Youth%20entrepreneurship%20 policy%20brief%20EN_FINAL.pdf; Terry Beech, Brenna Donoghue, Geordie Hungerford, Ali Okhowat, and Shannon Wells, *Fueling Canada's Economic Success: A National Strategy for High-Growth Entrepreneurship* (Action Canada, 2014), accessed November 2, 2014, http://www.actioncanada. ca/wp-content/uploads/2014/04/FuellingCanadasEconomicSuccess-ANationalStrategyForHigh-GrowthEntrepreneurship.pdf.

29 Carl J. Schramm, *The Entrepreneurial Imperative* (New York: Collins, 2006).
30 Brett A. Gilbert, David B. Audretsch, and Patricia P. McDougall, "The Emergence of Entrepreneurship Policy," *Small Business Economics* 22 (2004): 313–323.
31 Thom Rubel and Scott Palladino, *Nurturing Entrepreneurial Growth in State Economies* (Washington DC: National Governors' Association, 2000); Kyle Zinth, "Entrepreneurial Education Laws in the States," *StateNotes: Economic/Workforce Development* (Denver, CO: Education Commission of the States, 2007); British Columbia, *British Columbia's Technology Strategy: Building B.C.'s Economy* (Ministry of Jobs, Tourism, and Innovation, 2012); *The Innovative and Entrepreneurial University: Higher Education, Innovation, and Entrepreneurship in Focus* (US Department of Commerce, October 2013), accessed March 14, 2014, http://www.eda.gov/pdf/The_Innovative_ and_Entrepreneurial_University_Report.pdf; Ontario, *Seizing Global Opportunities: Ontario's Innovation Agenda* (Toronto, ON: Ministry of Research and Innovation, 2013).
32 William J. Kramer, Beth Jenkins, and Robert S. Katz, *The Role of the Information and Communications Technology Sector in Expanding Economic Opportunity* (The Fellows of Harvard College, 2007), accessed October 28, 2014, http://www.hks.harvard.edu/m-rcbg/CSRI/publications/ report_22_EO%20ICT%20Final.pdf.
33 Hoard E. Aldrich, "The Democratization of Entrepreneurship? Hackers, Makerspaces, and Crowdfunding," *Academy of Management Proceedings (Meeting Abstract Supplement)*, November 18, 2014, accessed December 1, 2014, http://proceedings.aom.org/content/2014/1/10622.short?related-urls=ye s&legid=amproc;2014/1/10622.
34 See Chapters 3 and 4.
35 See *The Global Consortium of Entrepreneurship Centers*, accessed November 30, 2014, https://www.globalentrepreneurshipconsortium.org:9443/index.cfm.

36 For an overview of the organization, see "History," *VentureWell*, accessed December 29, 2014, http://venturewell.org/history/.

37 "Background," *The Next 36*, accessed December 2, 2014, http://www.thenext36.ca/org/background.

38 *Startup Canada*, accessed December 2, 2014, http://www.startupcan.ca/.

39 Wendy E. F. Torrance. *Entrepreneurial Campuses: Action, Impact, and Lessons Learned from the Kauffman Campus Initiative* (Kansas City, MO: Ewing Marion Kauffman Foundation, August 2013).

40 *Coleman Fellows*, accessed December 2, 2014, https://colemanfellows.com/.

41 Matthew M. Mars, "The Diverse Agendas of Faculty Within An Institutionalized Model of Entrepreneurship Education," *Journal of Entrepreneurship Education* 10, no. 1 (2007): 43–62; Michael R. Bowers, C. M. Bowers, and Gabriel Ivan, "Academically-based Entrepreneurship Centers: An Exploration of Structure and Function," *Journal of Entrepreneurship Education* 9 (2006): 1–14; Todd A. Finkle, Teresa V. Menzies, Donald F. Kuratko, and Michael G. Goldsby, "Financial Activities of Entrepreneurship Centers in the United States," *Journal of Business and Entrepreneurship* 23, no. 2 (2012): 48–64.

42 Katz, *2004 Survey of Endowed Positions in Entrepreneurship and Related Fields in the United States*.

43 Teresa V. Menzies, "An Exploratory Study of University Entrepreneurship Centers in Canada," *Journal of Small Business and Entrepreneurship* 15, no. 3 (2000): 15–38.

44 Sophia Harris, "Entrepreneur Barbie Takes Aim at Glass Ceiling," *CBCNews*, July 9, 2014, accessed July 10, 2014, http://www.cbc.ca/m/touch/news/story/1.2701322.

45 Cooper H. Langford, Peter Josty, and J. Adam Holbrook, *Global Entrepreneurship Monitor: Canada National Report* (London, UK: Global Entrepreneurship Research Association, 2013).

46 Donna J. Kelley, Abdul Ali, Canadida Brush, Andrew Corbett, Mahdi Majbouri, and Edward Rogoff, *Global Entrepreneurship Monitor: United States National Report* (London, UK: Global Entrepreneurship Research Association, 2013).

47 George T. Solomon, Susan Duffy, and Ayman Tarabishy, "The State of Entrepreneurship Education in the United States: A Nationwide Survey and Analysis," *International Journal of Entrepreneurship Education* 1, no. 1 (2002): 65–86; Nancy M. Levenburg, Paul M. Lane, and Thomas V. Schwarz, "Interdisciplinary Dimensions in Entrepreneurship," *Journal of Education for Business* 81, no. 5 (2006): 275–281; Rachel Shinner, Mark Pruett, and Bryan Toney, "Entrepreneurship Education Attitudes Across Campus," *Journal of Education for Business* 84, no. 3 (2009): 151–158; Matthew J. Mayhew, Jeffrey S. Simonoff, William J. Baulmol, Batia M. Wiesenfeld, and Michael W. Klein,

"Exploring Innovative Entrepreneurship and Its Ties to Higher Educational Experiences," *Research in Higher Education* 53 (2012): 831–859.

48 John H. Pryor and E. J. Reedy, *Trends In Business Interest Among US College Students: An Early Exploration of Data Available From the Cooperative Institutional Research Program* (Kansas City, MO: Ewing Marion Kauffman Foundation, 2009), accessed August 5, 2014, http://papers.ssrn.com/sol3/papers.cfm?abstract_id=1971393.

49 Harris Interactive, *YouthPulseSM 2010: Kauffman Foundation Custom Report* (Kansas City, KS: Kauffman Foundation, 2010), accessed November 4, 2013, http://papers.ssrn.com/sol3/papers.cfm?abstract_id=1710013.

50 The Princeton Review, *2013 College hopes & worries survey report* (The Princeton Review, 2013), accessed November 19, 2014, http://www.princetonreview.com/uploadedFiles/Sitemap/Home_Page/Rankings/Hopes_and_Worries/2013/CollegeHopesandWorriesSurveyReport2013.pdf; Michele Serro, "The Schools of Hard Knocks: Can We Teach Entrepreneurship? *Huffington Post*, May 2, 2013, accessed September 1, 2014, http://www.huffingtonpost.com/michele-serro/the-school-of-hard-knocks-can-we-teach-entrepreneurship_b_3180393.html.

51 Geiger and Sá, *Tapping the Riches of Science*; Etkowitz, *MIT and the Rise of Entrepreneurial Science*; Sheila Slaughter and Gary Rhoades, *Academic Capitalism in the New Economy: Markets, State, and Higher Education* (Baltimore, MD: The John Hopkins University Press, 2005).

52 Geiger and Sá, *Tapping the Riches of Science*.

53 Scott A. Shane, *Academic Entrepreneurship: University Spinoffs and Wealth Creation* (Cheltenham, UK: Edward Elgar Publishing, 2004); Geiger and Sá, *Tapping the Riches of Science*.

54 Sheila Slaughter and Larry L. Leslie, *Academic Capitalism: Politics, Policies, and the Entrepreneurial University* (Baltimore, MD: The John Hopkins University Press, 1999); Slaughter and Rhoades, *Academic Capitalism in the New Economy*.

55 Raymond F. Zummuto, "Are the Liberal Arts an Endangered Species? *Journal of Higher Education* 55, no. 2 (1984): 184–211; Slaughter and Rhoades, *Academic Capitalism in the New Economy*.

56 Pierre Bourdieu, *Outline of a Theory of Practice,* trans. R. Nice (Cambridge, MA: Cambridge University Press, 1977); Pierre Bourdieu and Loïc J. D. Wacquant, *An invitation to Reflexive Sociology* (Chicago, IL: University of Chicago Press, 1992).

57 William B. Gartner and Karl H. Vesper, "Experiments in Entrepreneurship Education: Success and Failures," *Journal of Business Venturing* 9 (1994): 179–187; Jerome A. Katz, "Fully Mature But Not Fully Legitimate: A Different Perspective on the State of Entrepreneurship Education," *Journal of Small Business Management* 46, no. 4 (2008): 550–566; Donald F. Kuratko, "The Emergence of Entrepreneurship Education: Development, Trends, and

Challenges," *Entrepreneurship Theory and Practice* 29, no. 5 (2005): 577–598; George T. Solomon and Lloyd. W. Fernald Jr, "Trends in Small Business Management and Entrepreneurship Education in the United States. *Entrepreneurship Theory and Practice* 15, no. 3 (1991): 25–39.

# 2
# Entrepreneurship in North America

**Abstract:** *This chapter examines the scope of entrepreneurial activity in the United States and Canada, and provides evidence from which to gauge expectations surrounding entrepreneurs that underscore policy and institutional efforts to enhance the role of universities in stimulating entrepreneurship. The discussion in this chapter draws on a range of data pertaining to entrepreneurial attitudes, firm creation, employment generation, innovation, and technology transfer from universities. Survey data indicate that entrepreneurship is a widespread phenomenon that contributes to net employment gains in the US and Canadian economies. Higher education plays a role in the diffusion of entrepreneurship, as universities are increasingly contributing to the formation of new companies while graduates are more likely to start businesses in high-growth industries.*

Sá, Creso M. and Andrew J. Kretz. *The Entrepreneurship Movement and the University.* New York: Palgrave Macmillan, 2015. DOI: 10.1057/9781137401014.0005.

As discussed in Chapter 1, entrepreneurship is widely regarded as a powerful force driving innovation, productivity, job creation, and economic growth.[1] But just what is the scope of entrepreneurial activity in the United States and Canada? Is entrepreneurship, in practice, consistent with the lofty rhetoric around it? This chapter gauges the importance of entrepreneurial activity by drawing on a range of data from the two countries pertaining to entrepreneurial attitudes, firm creation, employment generation, innovation, and technology transfer from universities.

## Entrepreneurial attitudes and activity

The United States and Canada contain more entrepreneurial activity than other leading economies, and consistently rank high on most entrepreneurship indicators. In 2013, the percentage of the working population in the process of starting a business, or else managing a new one, was estimated at around 12–13 percent in Canada and the United States.[2] For comparison, in the United Kingdom early-stage entrepreneurs made up about seven percent of the working population, while in Germany, five percent of the population were engaged in start-up activity. Moreover, one-third of start-up creation takes place in new or emerging markets, which is a good indication of innovative entrepreneurial activity.[3] When compared to entrepreneurs in other developed economies, Americans and Canadians are more likely to engage in start-up activity by exploiting a marketable opportunity, rather than out of need for employment.

One near universal goal among proponents of technology-led economic development is the creation of an entrepreneurial culture. Such a culture presumes an inclination among the residents of a particular city, region, or country to engage in entrepreneurship, which is usually associated to the willingness to take risks and innovate. The lore of experts on entrepreneurship points to the United States as a particularly entrepreneurial nation, where entrepreneurs are celebrated, and failure in creating ventures does not carry a stigma.[4] Canada, on the other hand, is historically regarded as more risk averse—particularly in comparison to its southern neighbor.[5] These are of course broad generalizations, which overlook much variability across regions. Still, it is possible to draw on cross-national surveys that provide some clues as to the general attitudes regarding entrepreneurship in these two countries. One such source is the Global Entrepreneurship Monitor, which polled adults between the ages of 18 and 64 to assess entrepreneurial attitudes, activities, and aspirations. This survey shows that about 60 percent of adult Canadians agree that entrepreneurship is a good career choice, while 70 percent agree that successful entrepreneurs have high status. Moreover, respondents believe that the general media provides favorable coverage of entrepreneurs.[6] At the same time, nearly 14 percent of adults intended to start a new business venture. Interestingly and counterintuitively, this same survey shows that in the United States, only 12 percent of adults held entrepreneurial intention.[7]

Entrepreneurial intention is sensitive to economic conditions. As shown Figure 2.1, the number of people indicating that they planned to start a new business declined during the Great Recession, as would be expected given the adverse circumstances. Nonetheless, it has steadily increased ever since.[8] The percent of survey respondents reporting that they intended to start a new business has increased substantially since its low in 2008, extending to a high not even seen before the start of the Great Recession.

But how do those intentions translate into actual start-ups? It would seem clear that not all of those individuals who plan to create a new business actually see those plans through.

There are several ways to measure entrepreneurial activity, and one indicator used by the Global Entrepreneurship Monitor provides a

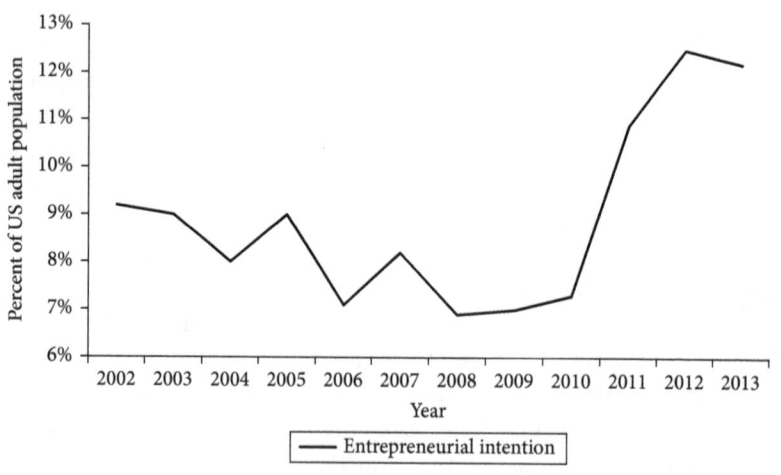

**FIGURE 2.1** *Entrepreneurial intentions in the United States*
Source: Global Entrepreneurship Monitor, *Adult Population Survey*.

response to the question above. The indicator is the "nascent entrepreneurship rate"— the proportion of the adult population involved in starting a new business. For 2013, the nascent entrepreneurship rate in the United States and Canada was estimated as 9.2 percent and 7.8 percent, respectively. In contrast to entrepreneurial aspirations, a larger share of the American population was engaged in start-up activity, as compared to their Canadian counterparts. Figure 2.2 shows the available data on this indicator over the last decade.

Another way to gain a sense of entrepreneurial activity is to take stock of the proportion of the workforce newly engaged in self-employment. In 2013, 0.28 percent of adults in the United States created a new business,[9] while in Canada about 1.35 percent of the workforce started a new business (see Figure 2.3).[10] From Figure 2.3 it can be seen that the US entrepreneurship rate slowly increased from its low in 2001 to a high of 0.34 at the end of the decade. In the last few years, the share of newly self-employed has receded to its 2006 rate. In Canada, there is no discernable trend in the rate of entrepreneurship since 2001. This observation follows previous research that found no clear trend in business entry rates in Canada between 2000 and 2008.[11] However, like in the United States, entrepreneurship rates have fallen since the end of the

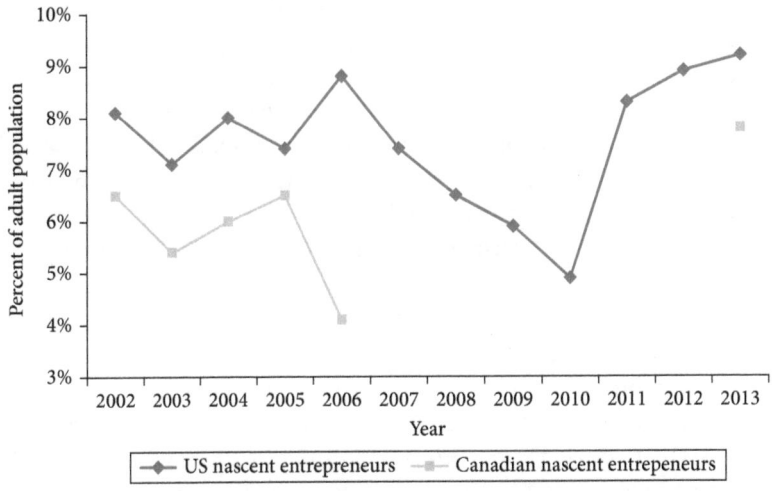

FIGURE 2.2  *Nascent entrepreneurship rates in the United States and Canada*
Note: Data for Canada for years 2007–2012 are not available.
Source: Global Entrepreneurship Monitor, *Adult Population Survey*.

24  *The Entrepreneurship Movement and the University*

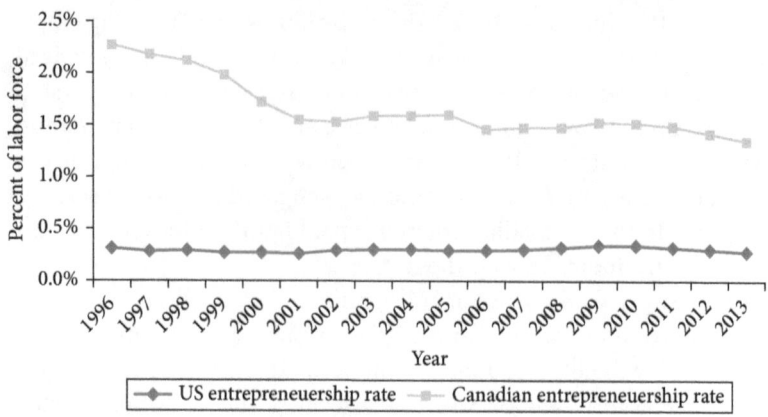

FIGURE 2.3   *Entrepreneurship rates in the United States and Canada*
Source:  Robert W. Fairlie, *Kauffman Index of Entrepreneurial Activity (KIEA)* (Kansas City, MO: Kauffman Foundation, 2014), using the *Current Population Survey*; Statistics Canada, *Labour Force Survey*.

Great Recession. Observing this trend in the United States, economist Robert W. Fairlie suggests that the weakened labor market during Great Recession exerted pressure toward self-employment, as opposed to the creation of companies that would generate jobs.[12]

To approximate the share of "opportunity" entrepreneurs—those individuals pursuing entrepreneurship to exploit a profitable opportunity, Fairlie calculated the share of entrepreneurs coming out of salaried employment and school, rather than unemployment. Individuals starting a business out of unemployment are often assumed to have done so as a condition of their unemployment, that is, they chose to start a business due to a lack of alternative employment opportunities.[13] This form of entrepreneurship is described as generally "replicative," because it is often based on the production or delivery of existing goods or services, rather than on the commercialization of new ideas, techniques, products, or services.[14] According to Fairlie, the proportion of entrepreneurs not starting a business out of unemployment was substantially higher before and after the Great Recession, indicating that the increase of self-employment during 2008–2011 was from individuals who had experienced unemployment. Notably, the share of total business creation by new entrepreneurs not coming out of unemployment has been generally declining over the past two decades, with peaks during times of general economic expansion, and troughs during economic contraction.[15]

Yet another way of illuminating the scope of entrepreneurship in the United States and Canada is to examine the number of new firms in each economy. Figure 2.4 shows the number of establishments in the United States born from firms that are less than a year old each year since 1977. The number of new establishments has stayed roughly between 500,000 and 600,000 each year. Better insight into the prevalence of entrepreneurship is had by measuring all establishments created by new companies in a given year as a proportion of new establishments created by existing firms. Figure 2.5 displays the percentage of new establishments

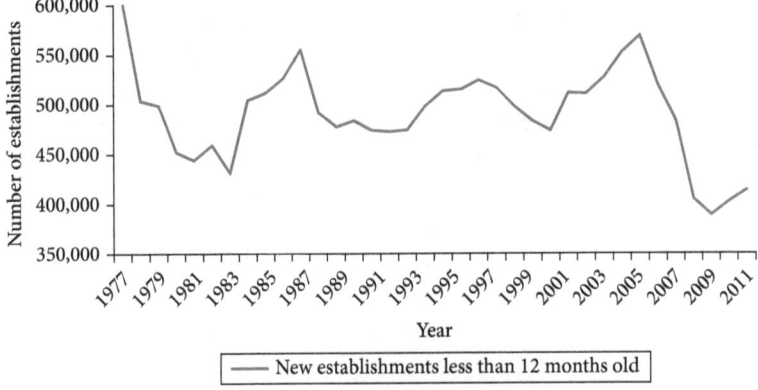

**FIGURE 2.4** *The number of establishments in the United States born from new firms*
*Source*: US Census Bureau, *Business Dynamics Statistics*.

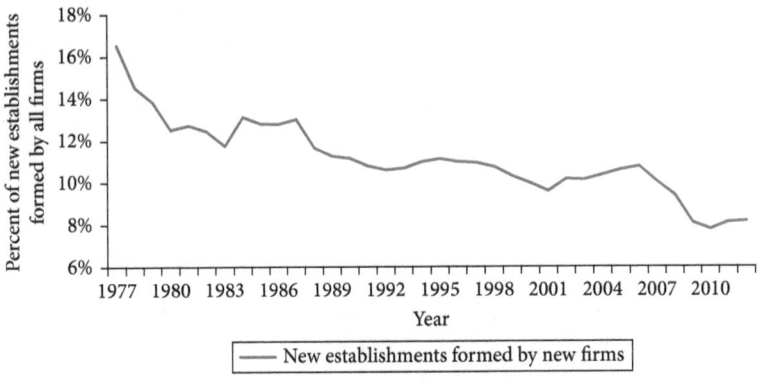

**FIGURE 2.5** *The percent of new establishments in the United States born from new firms*
*Source*: US Census Bureau, *Business Dynamics Statistics*.

from new firms as a percent of all new establishments by firms of all ages in the United States.[16] Notice the declining share of new establishments formed by new firms. A similar downward trend is apparent in the firm entry rate in Canada (see Figure 2.6).[17]

A large proportion of new companies in the United States and Canada never "scale-up," with many failing in the first few years after establishment.[18] About 15 percent of businesses fail in their first year, and another 15 percent do not survive past their second year. Survival rates of young companies continue to decline so that somewhere around 45 and 50 percent typically survive into their fifth year. Figure 2.7 illustrates this pattern by depicting the long-term survival rates of business establishments in the United States—a similar pattern is also observed in Canada.[19] High failure among new businesses is not restricted to "replicative" entrepreneurs or the newly self-employed, who may lack sufficient skills and resources to succeed. Even entrepreneurs with prepared business plans and large amounts of venture capital tend to struggle. One study of nearly 2,000 companies that received at least $1 million of venture funding revealed 30 to 40 percent of venture-backed start-ups fail to return investor's capital, while 70 to 80 percent fail to deliver their projected return on investment.[20]

Interestingly, while business entry rates tend to respond to growth opportunities in the broader economy, exit (or failure) rates tend to be "invariant to minor differences in economic climate."[21] In other words,

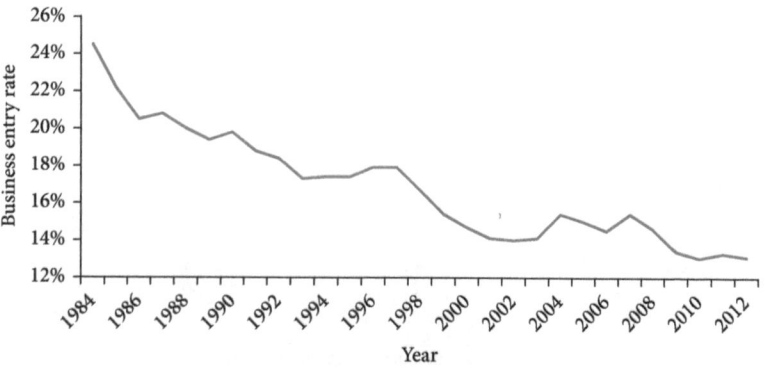

FIGURE 2.6   *The business entry rate in Canada*
Source:  Statistics Canada, *Longitudinal Employment Analysis Program (LEAP)*.

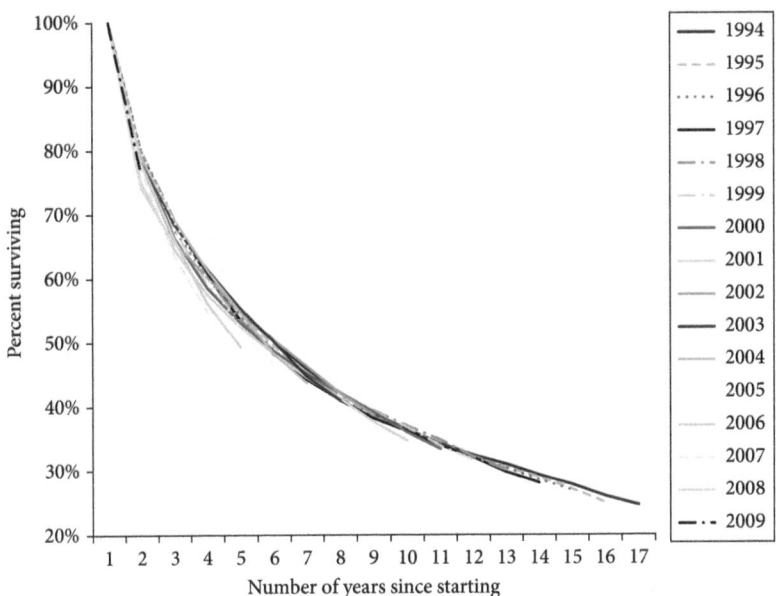

FIGURE 2.7 *Survival rates of US establishments, by year started and number of years since starting*

Source: US Bureau of Labor Statistics, *Business Employment Dynamics Data*.

the high exit rate for younger firms is emblematic of the risk, uncertainty, and experimentation inherent in business start-up. In fact, despite its negative connotation, failure has become a popularly celebrated and recognized reality of entrepreneurs. "Fail fast," "fail cheap," "fail better," and "fail forward" are popular mantras in entrepreneurship circles.[22] Eagerness to learning from the mistakes of others has even spawned a cottage industry. A number of conferences have been organized during which entrepreneurs convene to talk about their failed start-ups, and a Toronto consulting firm specializes in helping companies understand their failures.[23] At its core, the cult of failure is about embracing resiliency—the ability to learn and adapt from mistakes and forge ahead. The recognition of the likelihood that an entrepreneur will experience failure has been built into recipes for start-up development. For instance, the notion of "pivoting" as a shift in strategy is based on the notion that new ventures should learn from failures and apply these insights in new areas.[24]

## Start-ups and employment

Since the early 1980s, small firms have popularly been associated with contributing more to job creation than larger companies.[25] Recent scrutiny of the link between firm size and employment growth in the United States and Canada have revised this conventional wisdom by showing that business start-ups and young firms are key factors in job creation.[26] New firms have a higher job creation rate than older firms, and 40 percent of new hires at these young firms fill newly created jobs.[27] This ratio is much higher than in older firms, where it fluctuates between 25 and 33 percent.[28] Of course, new firms also have a higher job destruction rate (refer back to Figure 2.7).[29] Nevertheless, despite high rates of job destruction and firm failure, the difference between job creation and destruction, or their overall net job creation, is much higher for new firms than for older firms. In fact, start-up firms (those less than one year old) are responsible for all net job creation during most years in the United States, while existing firms (aged one year and older) are usually net job losers.[30]

Although younger firms are more likely than older firms to contribute to net job creation, the number of new employer businesses—those that provide work for individuals other than the founder—has been on the decline. Figure 2.6 showed that the start-up rate has declined from a high of 13 percent in the 1980s to below 8 percent in 2012. The rate of newly self-employed individuals that also hire employees shows a similar downward trend (see Figure 2.8).[31] However, rates of self-employed entrepreneurship and employer entrepreneurship differ. From 2011 to 2013, there has been a drop in self-employed entrepreneurship rates in the United States while employer business creation has increased. In Canada, the downward trend observed in self-employment is also evident for employer entrepreneurs. Interestingly, the difference in 2012 between US self-employed and employed is 0.17, while this ratio is 1.14 in Canada. These figures suggest that in comparison to US entrepreneurs, a larger number of Canadian entrepreneurs are self-employed—and presumably "replicative" entrepreneurs or else sole-proprietors.

The long-term decline of new business venture creation is also evident in the average share of net jobs created by start-ups. In the 1980s, start-ups created an average of 3.5 percent of net jobs annually, but only an average of 2.6 percent of net jobs annually in the 2000s. There is also an

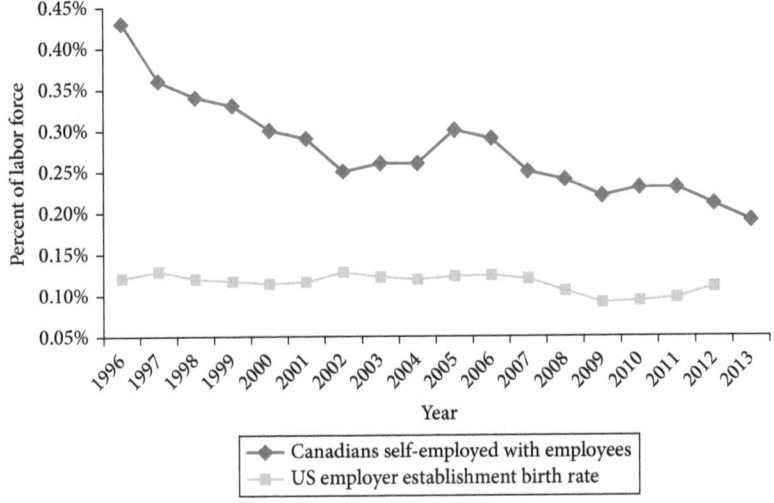

FIGURE 2.8  *Employer establishment birth rates in the United States and Canada*
Source: US Department of Labor, Bureau of Labor Statistics, *Business Employment Dynamics*; Statistics Canada, *Labour Force Survey*.

accompanying decline in the share of employment accounted for by new firms: it has fallen from more than 20 percent in the 1980s to as low as 12 percent in 2012. This trend of fewer hiring is also apparent in older firms.[32]

Although newer firms are largely responsible for gains in net employment, they do not generally offer higher paying jobs. There is a well-known and well-documented relationship between wages and firm size, and young firms—which tend to be relatively small in terms of number of employees—generally offer lower wages than at more mature firms. This difference persists across industry type. Moreover, the trend has been toward an even stronger relationship, as earnings have grown in large businesses while remaining stagnant or declining in small companies, and benefits in the latter are also lower.[33]

## Regional patterns

Entrepreneurial activity often depends on spatial proximity to knowledge sources—such as universities—and complementary industries. Proximity benefits entrepreneurs by making specialized infrastructure or access to a local labor market for specialized skills readily accessible.[34] The significance for entrepreneurs of proximity to ancillary activities and services, however, results from innovation being a geographically bounded phenomenon.[35] While "codified information" can be written down, transmitted, and understood by a recipient, proximity facilitates the exchange of "tacit knowledge." The tacit knowledge held by individuals with unique experience and know-how is typically geographically bounded, and its comprehension relates to local context and culture.[36] Effective transfer of tacit knowledge generally requires extensive personal contact and interaction. Proximity thus enhances the ability of entrepreneurs to exchange ideas and be cognizant of incipient knowledge formed from research and development activities.

Regions of intense technology-based entrepreneurship rely on various networks and forms of interaction that facilitate communication and information exchange.[37] The denser such regional networks become, the higher potential for local economic growth and development.[38] From this perspective, the region develops a unique milieu in which a complex web of relations and collective learning ties firms, customers, research institutions, and local authorities to each other.[39] This so-called "institutional thickness"—the "common industrial purpose and shared norms and values that serve to constitute 'the social atmosphere' of a particular locality"—helps drive economic development by cultivating a capacity to generate and assimilate innovation.[40] Indeed, entrepreneurs tend to thrive more when located within industrial clusters. Figures 2.9 and 2.10 show the geography of industrial agglomeration in two high-technology industries, biopharmaceutical and information technology/analytical instruments. Those regions in which these industries cluster, that is, where a relatively high number of companies colocate, tend to also have the most new firms in that industry. These examples help illustrate the relatively small number of regions that host a much higher than average-sized high-tech cluster.

Given the importance of proximity for innovation, entrepreneurial activity tends to agglomerate, or cluster, in various regions. The map in Figure 2.11 illustrates the dispersion of highly educated entrepreneurs across Canada and the United States in 2013. Although they appear distributed across the countries, pockets of entrepreneurship appear. Six metropolitan statistical areas are home to about 32 percent of all

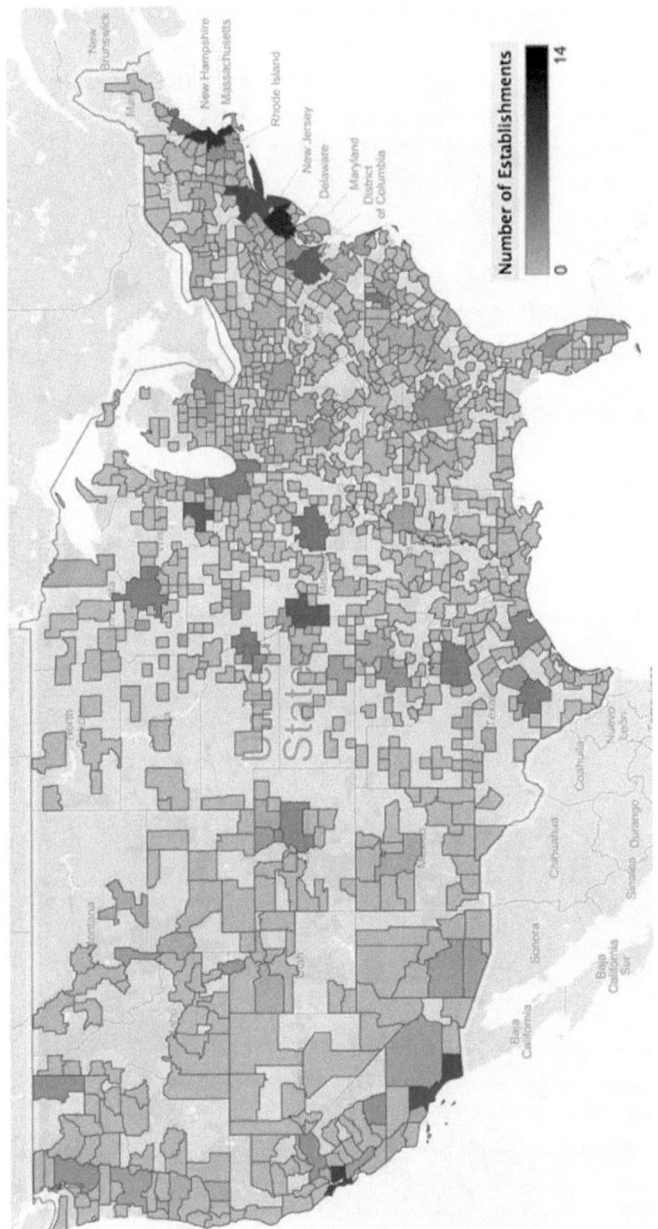

**FIGURE 2.9** *Biopharmaceutical establishments by MSA, 2012*
*Source:* Data from the US Cluster Mapping Project, Institute for Strategic and Competitiveness, Harvard Business School.

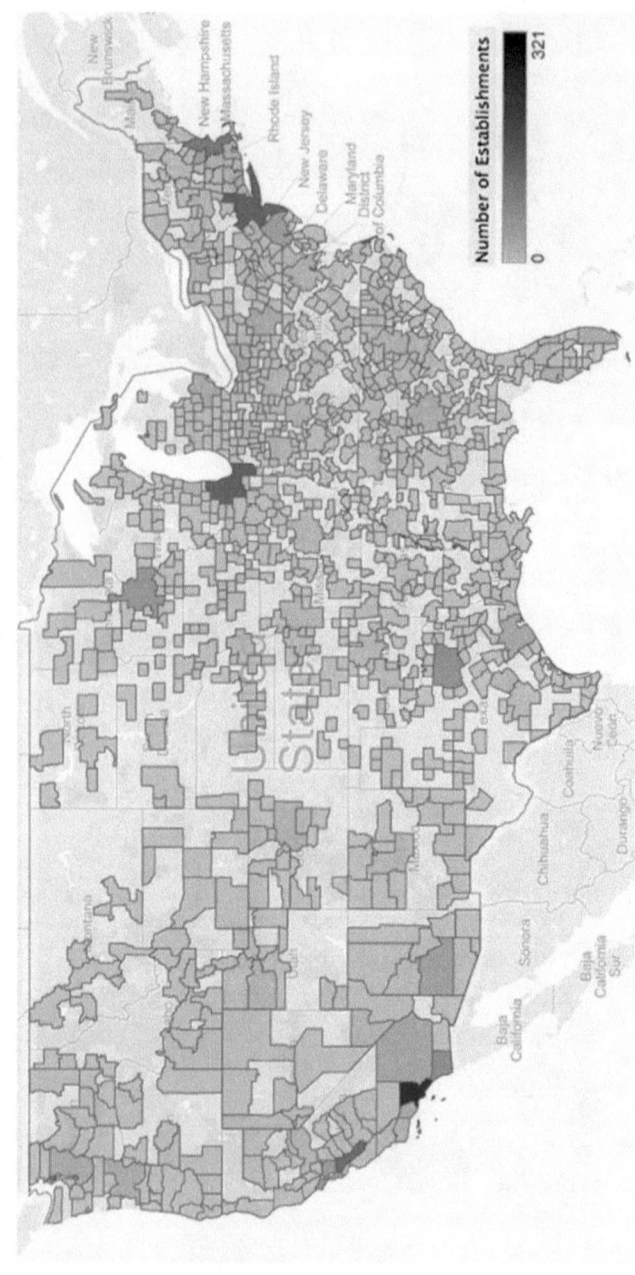

**FIGURE 2.10** *US Information technology and analytical instruments establishments by MSA, 2012*

*Source:* Data from the US Cluster Mapping Project, Institute for Strategic and Competitiveness, Harvard Business School.

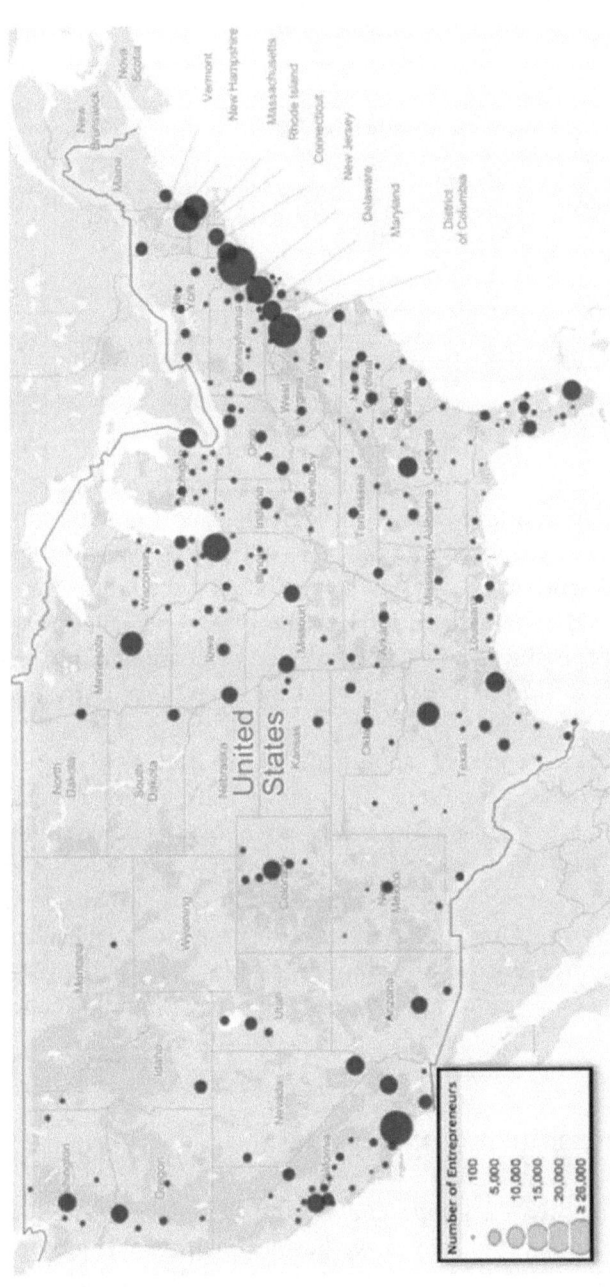

**FIGURE 2.11**  *Entrepreneurs in the United States, by MSA, 2013*

*Source:* Data from Robert W. Fairlie, *Kauffman Index of Entrepreneurial Activity (KIEA)* (Kansas City, MO: Kauffman Foundation, 2014), using the *Current Population Survey*.

TABLE 2.1  *Metropolitan statistical areas with the largest share of college or university educated entrepreneurs in professional, scientific, and technical services industries, 2013*

| Metropolitan statistical area | Percent |
|---|---|
| New York-Northern New Jersey-Long Island, NY-NJ | 6.9 |
| San Francisco-Oakland-Fremont, CA | 6.0 |
| Los Angeles-Long Beach-Santa Ana, CA | 5.6 |
| Washington-Arlington-Alexandria, DC-VA-MD | 5.6 |
| Philadelphia-Camden-Wilmington, PA-NJ-DE | 3.9 |
| Chicago-Naperville-Joliet, IN-IN-WI | 3.9 |
| Total | 31.9 |

Source: Robert W. Fairlie, *Kauffman Index of Entrepreneurial Activity (KIEA)* (Kansas City, MO: Kauffman Foundation, 2014). Data based on the Current Population Survey.

educated entrepreneurs in professional, scientific, or technical fields (Table 2.1). Provincial level data available for Canada provides a picture of regional variation in the vibrancy of entrepreneurial activity. Alberta had the largest net firm entry and the highest firm entry rate during the 2000s, while Atlantic Canada (New Brunswick, Prince Edward Island, Nova Scotia, and Newfoundland and Labrador) had the smallest net firm entry. The latter provinces suffer economic and demographic challenges. Quebec, one of the larger economies, had the lowest firm entry rate in the country.[41]

Canadian entrepreneurial activity is concentrated in its most populated provinces. When looking at newly self-employed working in professional, scientific, and technical fields, over 90 percent are in the four most densely populated provinces: Ontario (42.36), Quebec (22.42), British Columbia (13.87), and Alberta (13.10). Not surprisingly, Canada's largest metropolitan areas are home to a large number of educated entrepreneurs working in professional, scientific, or technical services: Toronto (24.27), Montreal (14.33), and Vancouver (9.40).

## Entrepreneurship and universities

Entrepreneurship that develops and commercializes new ideas and technologies disproportionately drive business activity and economic growth.[42] In order to successfully recognize and exploit potentially useful knowledge and technologies it is helpful for entrepreneurs to have the internal knowledge base and research capacity to acquire and apply research results.[43] Accordingly, several studies have found a positive association between an individual having attained a higher education degree and the likelihood of forming a business.[44] In 2013, 32 percent of US entrepreneurs and 33 percent of Canadian entrepreneurs held at least a four-year degree (see Figure 2.12). Moreover, in 2013, 12 percent of these highly educated entrepreneurs worked in professional, scientific, or technical service industries (see Figure 2.13). These are industries that are likely to rely on advanced knowledge and research cultivated in universities.

As sources of knowledge and new technology, universities are often catalysts of science-based innovation and entrepreneurship.[45] They are sources of expertise, inventions, and know-how that entrepreneurs can draw from to exploit venture opportunities.[46] Historically, university-based start-up companies have been formed around the innovative technologies resulting from faculty research. Traditional centers of university-based entrepreneurship include Stanford University and the Massachusetts Institute of Technology (MIT).[47] Over the last decade, more universities have embraced entrepreneurship as critical to their mission, and have subsequently spun-out an increasing number of new

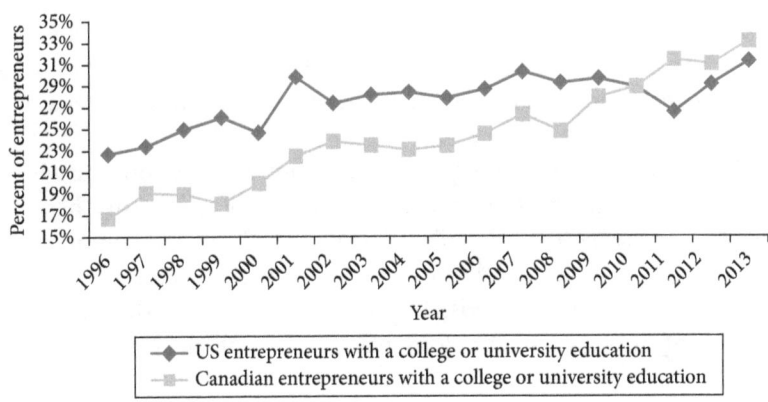

FIGURE 2.12  *Percent of entrepreneurs with a college or university education*

Source: Authors' calculations based on data from Robert W. Fairlie, *Kauffman Index of Entrepreneurial Activity (KIEA)* (Kansas City, MO: Kauffman Foundation, 2014) and Statistics Canada's *Labour Force Survey*.

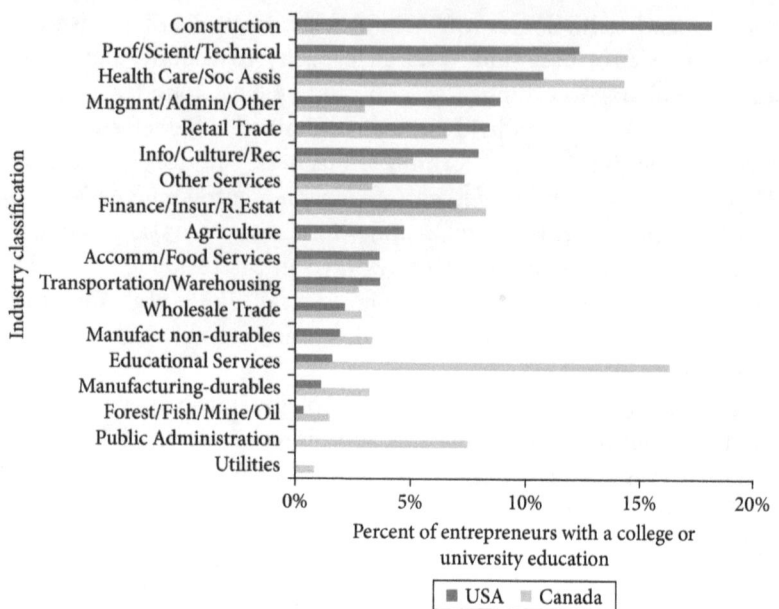

FIGURE 2.13   *Industries with entrepreneurs with a college or university education*

Source: Authors' calculations based on data from Robert W. Fairlie, *Kauffman Index of Entrepreneurial Activity (KIEA)* (Kauffman Foundation, Kansas City, MO, 2014) and Statistics Canada's *Labour Force Survey*.

companies based on university research. From 2001 to 2013, the rate of new companies initiated by university members of the Association of University Technology Managers' (AUTM) increased by an average of 4 percent per year (see Figure 2.14).

AUTM collects data from participating universities on start-up activity resulting from the commercialization of university-based intellectual property. Traditionally, these so-called spin-off companies are formed on the back of innovative technologies stemming from medical and engineering fields. Universities recently leading in the formation of university technology-based start-ups are presented in Table 2.2. Fourteen institutions, of those one based in Canada and four in California, have spun off 50 or more companies between 2009 and 2013.

These companies represent direct contribution to the local economy, as most university-based start-ups locate close to the university from which they originated.[48] From 2009 to 2013, nearly 78 percent of US

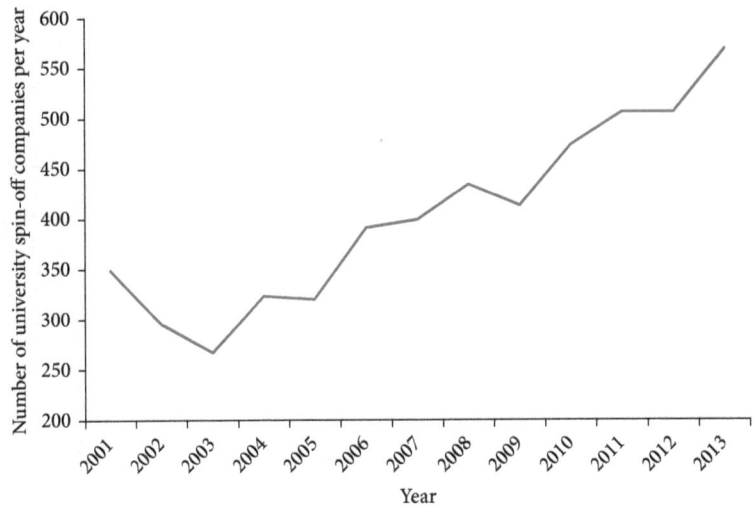

FIGURE 2.14   *University spin-off companies formed each year, 2001–2013*

*Note:* n = 74.

*Source*: Authors' calculations based on data from the Association of University Technology Managers (AUTM), *Licensing Activity Survey*.

university-based start-ups conducted most of their business in the state of their founding, while 84 percent of Canadian university-based start-ups conducted most of their business in the province of their founding.[49] For many new companies, proximity to universities brings advantages such as access to skilled labor, formal and informal technical support, specialized facilities, and experts.[50] Of course, proximity to the university is important for faculty members who start companies; they are likely to locate business close to their home university.[51] Considering these location patterns, Figure 2.15 illustrates the geographical distribution of university-related start-up activity in the United States and Canada based on the AUTM data on university spin-off companies.

Although promoting start-ups based on university research and intellectual property is now a well-established routine of universities, student entrepreneurship appears still in its nascency. In 2013, about 1 percent of Canadians enrolled at a university or college were entrepreneurs.[52] According to Statistics Canada surveys conducted over the 2000s, around 5 percent of Canadian postsecondary education graduates were self-employed two years after graduation.[53] Graduates from

TABLE 2.2  University spin-off companies created, by university from 2009 to 2013

| University | Number of spin-offs | University | Number of spin-offs |
|---|---|---|---|
| Univ. of Cal, Los Angeles[1] | 98 | Brigham Young Univ. | 37 |
| Univ. of Utah | 93 | Univ. of Cal, Berkeley | 36 |
| Massachusetts Inst. of Technology | 90 | Ohio State Univ. | 36 |
| Univ. of Toronto[2] | 77 | Univ. of Kentucky Research Foundation | 36 |
| Columbia Univ. | 69 | Univ. of North Carolina Chapel Hill | 36 |
| Univ. of Florida | 62 | New York Univ. | 35 |
| Univ. of Illinois at Chicago[3] | 60 | Univ. of New Mexico[7] | 34 |
| Univ. of Cal, San Diego | 60 | Univ. of Waterloo | 34 |
| Stanford Univ.[4] | 57 | Northwestern Univ. | 33 |
| CA Institute of Technology | 56 | Research Foundation of SUNY | 32 |
| Univ. of Pennsylvania | 56 | Univ. of Missouri | 31 |
| Carnegie Mellon Univ. | 52 | Univ. of Southern California | 30 |
| Univ. of Washington[5] | 52 | Duke Univ. | 29 |
| Georgia Inst. of Technology | 50 | Univ. of Pittsburgh | 29 |
| Univ. of Colorado | 49 | Univ. of Arizona | 29 |
| Univ. of Michigan | 49 | Rutgers Univ. | 28 |
| Johns Hopkins Univ. | 48 | Univ. of British Columbia | 28 |
| Indiana Univ.[6] | 46 | Penn State Univ. | 28 |
| Univ. of Minnesota | 46 | Univ. of Cal, San Francisco | 27 |
| Harvard Univ. | 44 | Univ. of Cal, Davis | 26 |
| University System of Maryland | 42 | Univ. of Texas, Austin[8] | 26 |
| Purdue Research Foundation | 41 | Texas A&M (system) | 25 |
| Cornell | 40 | Colorado State Univ. | 24 |
| Univ. of Nebraska | 40 | North Carolina State Univ. | 24 |
| Arizona State Univ. | 39 | Univ. of Cal, Irvine | 24 |

Notes: (1) Data for individual University of California campuses come from the University of California Technology Transfer Annual Reports. The University of California system reports to AUTM. (2) Excludes affiliated hospitals. (3) The University of Illinois data represents two of its largest campuses: Chicago and Urbana-Champaign. (4) AUTM does not contain 2012 data for Stanford University; we obtained the missing value by contacting Stanford University's TLO. (5) Includes activities from the Washington Research Foundation. (6) Includes activities from the Indiana University Advanced Research Technology Institute (ARTI). (7) Includes activities of STC.UTM (formerly known as the Science & Technology Corporation @ UNM). (8) AUTM does not contain 2013 data for the University of Texas, Austin.

DOI: 10.1057/9781137401014.0005

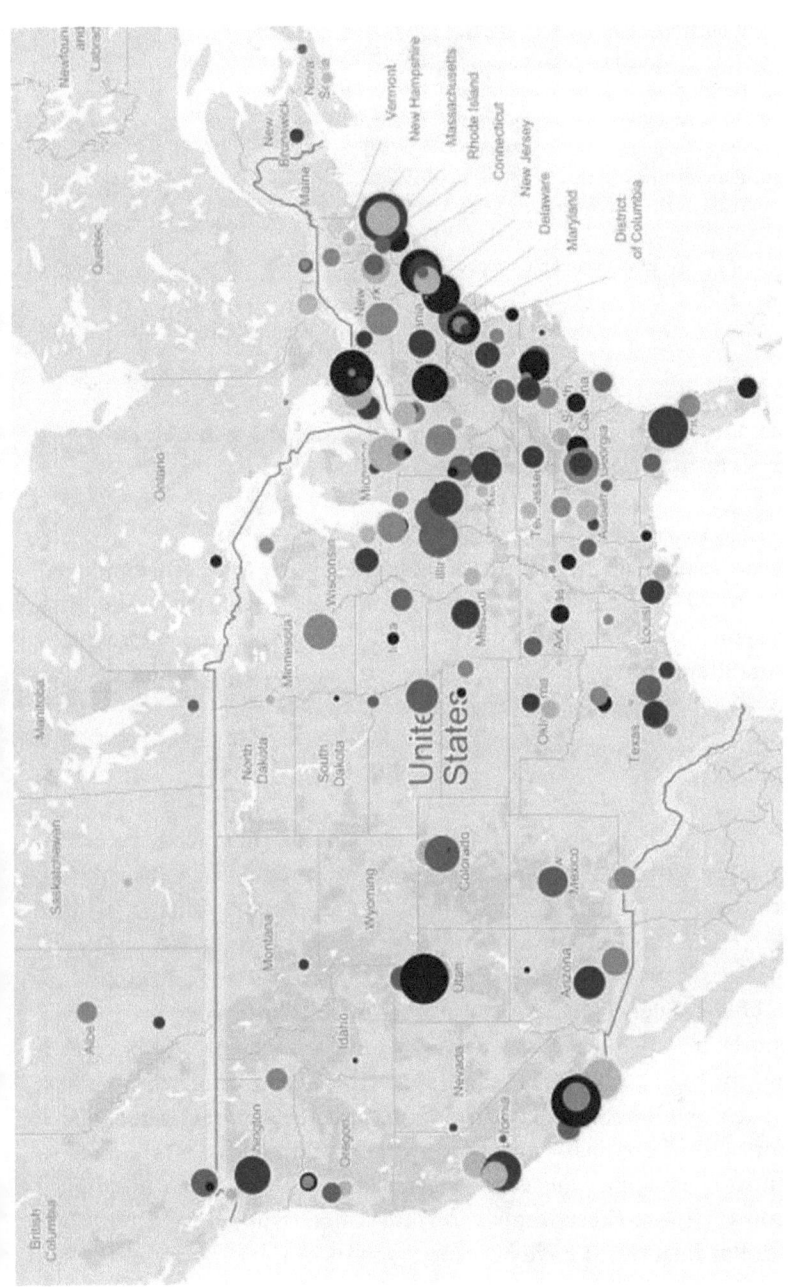

**FIGURE 2.15** *Location of university spin-off companies formed during 2009–2013*
*Source:* Authors' calculations based on data from the Association of University Technology Managers (AUTM), *Licensing Activity Survey.*

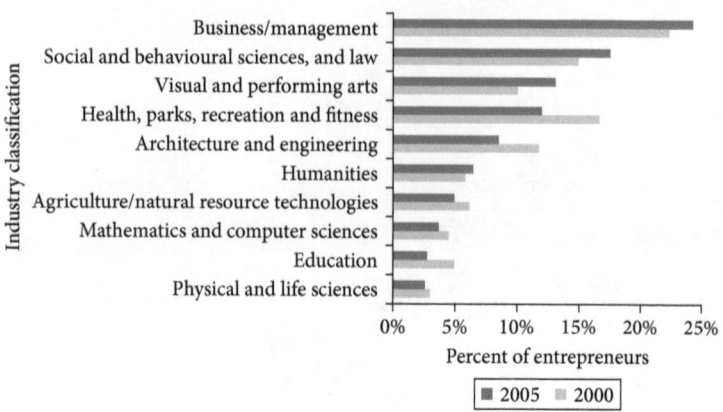

FIGURE 2.16  *Canadian entrepreneurs with a college or university education*
Source: Statistics Canada, *National Graduate Survey*.

business-related fields of study were the most likely to be self-employed, representing a quarter of all self-employed graduates. The self-employment rate among graduates from the physical and life sciences, and math and computer sciences, are among the lowest of all fields of study (see Figure 2.16).

\* \* \*

The United States and Canada are among the advanced industrial economies with the highest rates of entrepreneurial activity, and where positive attitudes prevail about entrepreneurs. This is in spite of persistent concerns in Canada about the country's perceived conservatism and risk-aversion when it comes to entrepreneurship. This concern seems to be fundamentally grounded in a direct comparison with the United States, which is a global reference as a hotbed of high-tech entrepreneurship. The question of why companies such as Google or Facebook were created in the United States and not elsewhere has been raised in many countries, in reference to the most spectacular successes of American companies in the digital economy.[54] These exceedingly rare cases of start-ups turned multibillion dollar businesses have become symbols of the capacity of the US universities to spur innovative firms.

As the next chapter will discuss, much faith has been posed in policy circles on the potential of entrepreneurship to address problems such as unemployment and economic revitalization. Although start-ups and young firms are responsible for a significant share of net job creation, the attribution of job creation to entrepreneurs arises largely from relatively large job losses in older firms. Overall, start-ups do not generate especially large increases in the number of jobs available. In fact, the declining percentage of job creation by start-ups and young firms indicates that start-ups alone cannot solve underemployment problems.

However, as an inherently localized phenomenon, entrepreneurship can contribute to the economic vibrancy of those places where an entrepreneurial climate prevails and start-ups flourish. Among the contributions of universities to innovation, nurturing new companies is one of the most likely to help the local and regional economy. Universities have been expected to generate growing numbers of start-ups firms, as the next two chapters will show. New ventures can bring resources to the campus where they originate, and if successful, can contribute to the local economy. Such start-up companies may be the vehicles through which university research or the invention of students is commercialized.[55] These reasons underscore policy and institutional efforts to enhance the role of universities in stimulating entrepreneurial activity.

# Notes

1. Zoltan J. Acs, "How is Entrepreneurship Good for Economic Growth?" *Innovations* 1, no. 1 (2006): 97–107.
2. Cooper H. Langford, Peter Josty, and J. Adam Holbrook, *Global Entrepreneurship Monitor: Canada National Report* (Global Entrepreneurship Monitor, 2013); Donna J. Kelley, Abdul Ali, Canadida Brush, Andrew Corbett, Mahdi Majbouri, and Edward Rogoff, *Global Entrepreneurship Monitor: United States National Report* (Global Entrepreneurship Monitor, 2013).
3. Langford et al., *Global Entrepreneurship Monitor: Canada National Report*; Kelley et al., *Global Entrepreneurship Monitor: United States National Report*.
4. Kevin Roose, "The Failure Fetish in Silicon Valley," *New York Magazine*, March 24, 2014, accessed November 1, 2014, http://nymag.com/daily/intelligencer/2014/03/silicon-valley-failure-fetish.html. Coverage of

entrepreneurial climates in other countries typically defer to the US culture of celebrating failure. See for instance, Peter Gumbel, "To Boost Entrepreneurship, France Tries to Change Its Attitude toward Failure," *Reuters*, January 23, 2014, accessed November 1, 2014, http://blogs.reuters.com/great-debate/2014/01/23/to-boost-entrepreneurship-france-tries-to-change-its-attitude-toward-failure/.

5   See for example, *A Path Forward for Entrepreneurship in Canada* (Canadian Chamber of Commerce, September 2014).
6   Langford et al., *Global Entrepreneurship Monitor: Canada National Report*.
7   Kelley et al., *Global Entrepreneurship Monitor: United States National Report*.
8   Entrepreneurial intentions represent the percentage of individuals who expect to start a business within three years of being surveyed.
9   Estimates calculated by Robert W. Fairlie, *Kauffman Index of Entrepreneurial Activity (KIEA)* (Kansas City, MO: Kauffman Foundation, 2014) using the Current Population Survey, which is sponsored jointly by the US Census Bureau and the US Bureau of Labor Statistics. The entrepreneurship index is the percent of individuals (aged 20–64) who do not own a business in the first survey month that start a business in the following survey month (a year later) with 15 or more hours worked. All observations with allocated (imputed) labor force status, class of worker, and hours worked variables are excluded from figures produced from KIEA data. For a detailed discussion of the data and methods underlying the KIEA, see Fairlie, *Kauffman Index of Entrepreneurial Activity (KIEA)* (2005).
10  Estimates are calculated from Statistics Canada's Labour Force Survey (LFS), which is a monthly survey of a sample of households, and includes civilian workers and unemployed individuals actively looking for a job who are 15 years of age or older. Individuals who became self-employed within the 12 months proceeding the survey are considered here as entrepreneurs. All inconsistent or missing information are allocated by Statistics Canada. The Business Development Bank of Canada has used this measure to previously assess entrepreneurship rates in Canada. See *BDC Index of New Entrepreneurial Activity 2012* (Business Development Bank of Canada, 2012).
11  This study was based on the number of firms created annually, see Oana Ciobanu and Weimin Wang, "Firm Dynamics: Firm Entry and Firm Exit in Canada, 2000–2008," *The Canadian Economy in Transition*, no. 022. Statistics Canada Catalogue no. 11–622-M (Ottawa: Statistics Canada, 2012).
12  According to Fairlie, "[t]hese individuals were probably more likely to start sole proprietorships and other non-employer firms instead of more costly employer firms" [Fairlie, *Kauffman Index of Entrepreneurial Activity* (2013), 6].
13  Zóltan J. Acs and Attila Varga, "Agglomeration, Entrepreneurship and Technological Change," *Small Business Economics* 24, no. 2 (2005): 323–334.

14. William J. Baumol, Robert E. Litan, and Carl J. Schramm, *Good Capitalism, Bad Capitalism, and The Economics of Growth and Prosperity* (New Haven, CT: Yale University Press, 2007).
15. Fairlie, *Kauffman Index of Entrepreneurial Activity* (2013).
16. The Business Dynamics Statistics (BDS) provides annual measures of business dynamics (such as job creation and destruction, establishment births and deaths, and firm start-ups and shutdowns). The BDS is created from the Census Bureau's Longitudinal Business Database. Establishments are used in the tabulation of the BDS statistics. An establishment is a fixed physical location where economic activity occurs. A firm may have one establishment (a single–unit establishment) or many establishments (a multi–unit firm). Firms are defined at the enterprise level such that all establishments under the operational control of the enterprise are considered part of the firm. The BDS does not include nonemployer firms and, as such, this brief does not speak to job creation from nonemployer businesses.
17. The Longitudinal Employment Analysis Program (LEAP) is a database that contains annual employment information for each employer business in Canada. The information in LEAP is generated from the annual statements of remuneration paid (T4 slips) that Canadian businesses are required to issue to their employees for tax purposes. LEAP covers incorporated and unincorporated businesses that issue at least one T4 slip in any given calendar year, but excludes self-employed individuals or partnerships where the participants do not draw salaries.
18. Industry Canada, *Key Small Business Statistics* (Ottawa: Industry Canada, 2012); US Census Bureau, *Business Development Statistics* (2012), http://www.census.gov/ces/dataproducts/bds/; Ryan Macdonald, "Firm Dynamics: The Death of New Canadian Firms: A Survival Analysis of the 2002 Cohort of Entrants to the Business Sector," *The Canadian Economy in Transition Series*, Catalogue no. 11–622-M, no. 028 (Ottawa: Statistics Canada, 2012).
19. Industry Canada, *Key Small Business Statistics*.
20. Deborah Gage, "The Venture Capital Secret: 3 Out of 4 Start-Ups Fail," *The Wall Street Journal*, September 20, 2012, accessed October 4, 2014, http://online.wsj.com/articles/SB10000872396390443720204578004980476429190.
21. John R. Baldwin, Huju Liu, and Weimin Wang, "Firm Dynamics: Firm Entry and Exit in the Canadian Provinces, 2000 to 2009," *The Canadian Economy in Transition Series*, Catalogue no. 11–622-M, no. 030 (Ottawa: Statistics Canada, 2013).
22. See Anjali Sastry and Kara Penn, *Fail Better: Design Smart Mistakes and Succeed Sooner* (Boston, MA: Harvard Business Review Press, 2014).
23. Claire Martin, "Wearing Your Failures on Your Sleeve," *The New York Times*, November 8, 2014, accessed November 10, 2014, http://www.nytimes.com/2014/11/09/business/wearing-your-failures-on-your-sleeve.html.

24  Steve Blank, "Why the Lean Start-up Changes Everything," *Harvard Business Review* 91, no. 5 (2013): 63–72.
25  David L. Birch, "Who Creates Jobs?" *The Public Interest* 65 (1981): 3–14.
26  Jay Dixon and Anne-Marie Rollin, "Firm Dynamics: Employment Growth Rates of Small Versus Large Firms in Canada," *The Canadian Economy in Transition* (11-622-M), no. 25, (Ottawa: Ministry of Industry, 2012); Haltiwanger, J., R. S. Jarmin, and J. Miranda, "Who Creates Jobs? Small Versus Large Versus Young?" *The Review of Economics and Statistics* 45, no. 2 (2013): 347–361; Tim Kane, "The Importance of Startups in Job Creation and Job Destruction," *Kauffman Foundation Research Series: Firm Formation and Economic Growth* (Kansas City, MO: Kauffman Foundation, 2010); Jason Wiens and Chris Jackson, "The Importance of Young Firms for Economic Growth," *Entrepreneurship Policy Digest* (Kansas City, MO: Kauffman Foundation, September 25, 2014).
27  Employer firms in the first two years of operation.
28  John Haltiwanger, Henry Hyatt, Erika McEntarfer, and Liliana Sousa, "Job Creation, Worker Churning, and Wages at Young Businesses," *Business Dynamics Statistics Briefing* (Kansas City, MO: Kauffman Foundation, 2012).
29  Haltiwanger et al., "Job Creation, Worker Churning, and Wages at Young Businesses." In Canada, this phenomenon is evidenced by the positive correlation between firm entry and exit rates. See Baldwin et al., "Firm Dynamics: Firm Entry and Exit in the Canadian Provinces, 2000 to 2009."
30  Haltiwanger et al., "Job Creation, Worker Churning, and Wages at Young Businesses."
31  The employer establishment birth rate is the ratio of the average number of establishment births divided by the average number of nonbusiness owners. Data for the United States are from Business Employment Dynamics Data, a set of statistics generated from the Quarterly Census of Employment and Wages program. According to Fairlie (2014), Business Employment Dynamics data indicate roughly the same number of new businesses per year as the KIEA. Canadian data are calculated from Statistics Canada's LFS.
32  Haltiwanger, J., R. S. Jarmin, and J. Miranda, "Where Have All the Young Firms Gone?"; Dane Stangler and Paul Kedrosky, "Neutralism and Entrepreneurship: The Structural Dynamics of Startups, Young Firms, and Job Creation," *Kauffman Foundation Research Series: Firm Formation and Economic Growth* (Kansas City, MO: Kauffman Foundation, 2010); Robert Litan and E. J. Reedy, "Starting Smaller; Staying Smaller: America's Slow Leak in Job Creation," *Kauffman Foundation Research Series: Firm Formation and Economic Growth* (Kansas City, MO: Kauffman Foundation, 2010); Haltiwanger et al., "Job Creation, Worker Churning, and Wages at Young Businesses."

33 Haltiwanger et al., "Job Creation, Worker Churning, and Wages at Young Businesses;" Adam Seth Litwin and Phillip H. Phan, "Quality over Quantity: Reexamining the Link between Entrepreneurship and Job Creation," *Industrial Relations and Labor Review* 66, no. 4 (2013): 833 – 873; Dixon and Rollin, "Firm Dynamics: Employment Growth Rates of Small Versus Large Firms in Canada."
34 Michael E. Porter, *The Competitive Advantage of Nations* (New York: Free Press, 1990).
35 David B. Audretsch and Maryann P. Feldman, "R&D Spillovers and the Geography of Innovation and Production," *The American Economic Review* 86, no. 3 (1996): 630–640; Jeremy R. L. Howells, "Tacit Knowledge, Innovation and Economic Geography," *Urban Studies* 39 (2002): 871–884; Adam B. Jaffe, Manuel Trajtenberg, and Rebecca Henderson, "Geographic Localization of Knowledge Spillovers as Evidenced by Patent Citations," *The Quarterly Journal of Economics* 108 (1993): 577–598; Maryann P. Feldman, "The New Economics of Innovation, Spillovers and Agglomeration: A Review of Empirical Studies," *The Economics of Innovation and New Technology* 8 (1999): 5–25; Maryann P. Feldman and David B. Audretsch, "Innovation in Cities: Science-Based Diversity, Specialisation, and Localised Competition," *European Economic Review* 43 (1999): 409–429.
36 Michael Polanyi, *The Tacit Dimension* (New York: Doubleday, 1966); Meric Gertler, "Tacit Knowledge and the Economic Geography of Context, or the Undefinable Tacitness of Being (There)," *Journal of Economic Geography* 3, no. 1 (2003): 75–99.
37 Giovanni Dosi, "Sources, Procedures and Microeconomic Effects of Innovation," *Journal of Economic Literature* 26 (1988): 1120–1171; Philip Cooke, "Regional Innovation Systems, Clusters and the Knowledge Economy," *Industrial and Corporate Change* 10 (2001): 945–974; Feldman and Audretsch, "Innovation in Cities: Science-Based Diversity, Specialisation, and Localised Competition"; Michael Storper, "The Resurgence of Regional Economies, Ten Years Later: The Region As a Nexus of Untraded Interdependencies," *European Urban and Regional Studies* 2 (1995): 191–221.
38 Ash Amin and N. Thrift, "Globalization, Institutional Thickness and the Local Economy," in *Managing Cities: The New urban Context*, eds. Healy P., Cameron S., and Davoudi A. (Chichester, UK: John Wiley, 1995), 91–108; Philip Cooke and Kevin Morgan, *The Associational Economy: Firms, Regions and Innovation* (Oxford: Oxford University Press, 1998); Maryann P. Feldman and Ted D. Zoller, "Dealmakers in Place: Social Capital Connections in Regional Entrepreneurial Economies," *Regional Studies* 46, no. 1 (2012): 23–37.
39 W. J. Coffey and A. Bailly, "Economic Restructuring: A Conceptual Framework," in *The Spatial Impact of Economic Change in Europe*, eds. William F. Lever and Antoine Bailly (Aldershot: Avebury, 1996), 13–39; Denis

Maillat, "Territorial Dynamic, Innovative Milieus and Regional Policy," *Entrepreneurship & Regional Development* 7, no. 2 (1995): 157–165.

40  Amin and Thrift, "Globalization, Institutional Thickness and the Local Economy," 104.

41  Baldwin et al., "Firm Dynamics: Firm Entry and Exit in the Canadian Provinces, 2000 to 2009."

42  Matthew D. Regele and Heidi M. Neck, "The Entrepreneurship Education Sub-Ecosystem in the United States: Opportunities to Increase Entrepreneurial Activity," *Journal of Business & Entrepreneurship* 23, no. 2 (2012): 25–47.

43  Wesley M. Cohen and Daniel A. Levinthal, "Absorptive Capacity: A New Perspective on Learning and Innovation," *Administrative Science Quarterly* 35 (1990): 128–152; Attila Varga, "Universities and Regional Economic Development: Does Agglomeration Matter?" in *Theories of Endogenous Regional Growth—Lessons for Regional Policies*, eds. Börje Johansson, Charlie Karlsson, and Roger Stough (Berlin: Springer, 2001), 345–367.

44  Chad M. Moutray, "Educational Attainment and Other Characteristics of the Self-Employed: An Examination using Data from the Panel Study of Income Dynamics," *Hudson Institute Research Paper* no. 07–06 (2007), accessed September 4, 2014, http://papers.ssrn.com/sol3/papers.cfm?abstract_id=1070835.

45  Jérôme Doutriaux, "University-Industry Linkages and the Development of Knowledge Clusters in Canada," *Local Economy* 18 no. 1 (2003): 63–79.

46  David B. Audretsch, "The Knowledge Spillover Theory of Entrepreneurship and Economic Growth," *Research on Technological Innovation, Management and Policy* 9 (2005): 37–54.

47  Roger L. Geiger and Creso Sá, *Tapping the Riches of Science: Universities and the Promise of Economic Growth* (Cambridge, MA: Harvard University Press, 2008).

48  Scott Shane, *Academic Entrepreneurship: University Spinoffs and Wealth Creation* (Cheltenham, UK: Edgar Elgar Publishers, 2004).

49  Data are from the Association of University Technology Managers' (AUTM) Statistics Access for Tech Transfer database, which contains data from AUTM's annual Licensing Activity Survey.

50  Allison Bramwell and David A. Wolfe, "Universities and Regional Economic Development: The Entrepreneurial University of Waterloo," *Research Policy* 37, no. 8 (2008): 1175–1187.

51  Janet Bercovitz and Maryann Feldman, "Entrepreneurial Universities and Technology Transfer: A Conceptual Framework for Understanding Knowledge-Based Economic Development," *The Journal of Technology Transfer* 31, no. 1 (2006): 175–188.

52  These percentages are likely inflated, as some survey respondents may have started a venture and then enrolled at a university or college.

53  Data based on Statistics Canada's *National Graduate Survey* (2005, 2007).
54  See, for instance, "European Entrepreneurs: Les Misérables," *The Economist*, July 28, 2012, accessed December 10, 2014, http://www.economist.com/node/21559618.
55  Geiger and Sá, *Tapping the Riches of Science*.

# 3
# Public Policy for Entrepreneurship

**Abstract:** *Federal, state, and provincial governments have become increasingly involved in nurturing entrepreneurs, particularly those working in technology-based sectors. Universities themselves have assumed a key position in entrepreneurship policy. This chapter examines contemporary policy efforts to make universities anchors of regional entrepreneurial ecosystems. These initiatives follow from national science, technology, and innovation agendas, and harbour expectations to address competitiveness challenges and employment needs. At the state and provincial level, universities have come to the forefront over the last few decades in policies supporting high-tech entrepreneurship, and initiatives dealing with entrepreneurship have become part of the expectations of policymakers. Public policies are an important source of funding for entrepreneurship programs and help to encourage and legitimize entrepreneurial learning and practice in universities.*

Sá, Creso M. and Andrew J. Kretz. *The Entrepreneurship Movement and the University.* New York: Palgrave Macmillan, 2015. DOI: 10.1057/9781137401014.0006.

All levels of government in North America have promoted high-tech entrepreneurship. The role of the federal governments in the United States and Canada in stimulating venture creation is well established. State and provincial governments have become increasingly involved in nurturing entrepreneurship as well, as every region has aspired to grow a "cluster" in a technology-based sector.[1] Universities themselves have assumed a key position in policy in this area. Academic institutions outside of established entrepreneurial hubs are becoming heavily invested in fostering new entrepreneurial ecosystems, and are increasingly receiving support from governments to stimulate entrepreneurial activity. This chapter examines these contemporary policy efforts to make entrepreneurship at universities anchors of regional venture creation and cluster building.

## Evolving government roles

Generic support for business creation in both Canada and the United States is longstanding. In both countries, new business creation has been generally promoted with changes to business regulations, taxation, and training. Nonetheless, the roles that governments have played have evolved considerably since the mid-twentieth century. At the national level, the ethos of assisting fragile small businesses prevailed until around 1980, when it began to be replaced by the view that entrepreneurial start-ups could be the vehicle for innovation. Since then, federal governments in both countries have through federal agencies and targeted programs sought to support R&D and technology commercialization activities involving new firms. Part of this support flows through institutions that historically supported small business owners; part through research funding agencies that support academic science.

Representative of these evolving roles are the early economic institutions focused on small businesses. The Business Development Bank of Canada was founded in 1944 (as the Industrial Development Bank) to finance the development of national industry, and added consulting and training services to its financial offerings in the mid-1970s. In 1995, the Canadian Parliament passed the Business Development Bank of Canada Act, mandating BDC to promote entrepreneurship, with a special focus on the needs of small and medium-sized enterprises.[2] In the United States, the 1953 Small Business Act created the Small Business

Administration, whose function was to "aid, counsel, assist and protect, insofar as is possible, the interests of small business concerns." Since the mid-1970s, the SBA has supported connections between universities and small business development.[3] The focus on helping entrepreneurs is reflected in the Office of Entrepreneurial Development (OED), which oversees a network of programs and services that support the training and counselling needs of small businesses. Moreover, the Office of Entrepreneurship Education specializes on the provision of training resources and programs for business owners or those wishing to start a new company.[4] Another longstanding institution is Canada's Industrial Research Assistance Program (IRAP), which has connected small and mid-sized enterprises with universities, colleges, and other research institutions in order to improve innovative capacity and product commercialization.[5]

Explicit policy support for start-ups became an important strategy during the 1990s, as entrepreneurs were viewed as the key agents for generating economic growth and employment.[6] Underlying these policy efforts is the recognition of knowledge as a key source of economic competitiveness for firms and regions. Policymakers have sought to create environments that stimulate entrepreneurs to engage in knowledge-intensive start-up activity.[7] Support for such entrepreneurs generally falls under various policy initiatives involving funding for R&D, intellectual property, and university-industry collaboration.[8] The allure of entrepreneurs has stimulated policy debate in a range of areas, including science & technology, R&D, business financing, and immigration. Entrepreneurship became a viable "policy solution" for several issues in national economic and employment debates.[9] As a result, the two countries have moved to support high-tech entrepreneurship more deliberately at the federal level, seeking to spur innovative, technology-based start-ups (see section below).

At the state and provincial level, a long-term shift in strategies to foster regional economic development has brought university start-ups to the forefront. Historically, a large portion of knowledge-intensive entrepreneurial activity has been clustered within a small number of regions, such as San Francisco/Silicon Valley and Greater Boston in the United States. These well-known, and heavily studied hubs of entrepreneurship are home to many of the most successful technologically innovative companies in the world. Universities have been central to entrepreneurial development in these regions. Numerous faculty and students associated with Stanford University, for instance, are famously associated with the rise of companies that include Cisco Systems, Hewlett-Packard Company, Sun Microsystems, Google and Yahoo.[10] The roles of universities in the production of basic and applied research, transferring knowledge, and attracting talent contributed to the development of these entrepreneurial hubs. As much as the conditions leading to the spectacular successes of Stanford and MIT are unique, they have become powerful exemplars in the collective imaginary of policy makers, university administrators, and economic development professionals.[11] Other well-regarded cases of university-industry collaboration and entrepreneurship emerged in areas such as the Research Triangle in North Carolina and the Waterloo-Kitchener region in Ontario. In those regions, steps were taken in the late 1950s and early 1960s to revamp local economies with the participation of universities, providing a blueprint for governments and universities of close engagement in fostering entrepreneurial environments.[12]

During the last four decades, state and provincial governments moved from the older reliance on the industrial recruitment approach to regional economic development to the entrepreneurial approach.[13] Derided as "smokestack chasing," industrial recruitment involves providing incentives for large firms to relocate to a particular region, with the expectation that job creation will overtime offset the subsidies provided. The entrepreneurial approach focuses instead on growing new companies and stimulating regional industries to develop. As the thinking around how best to support regional economies evolved during the 1980s and 1990s, the popularization of the idea of high-tech "clusters" created a "Holy Grail" for economic development officials. A proliferation of entrepreneurial "zones," "routes," and "valleys" has occurred ever since, with claims that such regions excel in some particular technological niche.[14]

Although entrepreneurship policies have not completely replaced industrial recruitment, and sometimes both occur in the same region,[15] the entrepreneurial approach has become the contemporary conventional wisdom. Entrepreneurial policies at the state and provincial level can be differentiated between those focusing "upstream", or in the S&T infrastructure, or "downstream", on commercialization and venture creation.[16] Upstream policies involve investments in university research, cutting-edge laboratories, and research chairs in targeted technological fields. These investments build long-term technological capacity in the region. Downstream programs focus more directly on entrepreneurs and start-up companies, providing assistance for the development and commercialization of innovations. They involve creating business incubators and accelerators, funding innovation projects involving start-ups, and providing business assistance to high-tech ventures. Arguably, stimulating high-tech entrepreneurship involves both upstream and downstream approaches. University inventions that might lead to venture creation in science-based technologies (e.g. ICT, biotechnology, nanotechnology) relate to the nature of the research taking place on campus, as well as the quality of the research infrastructure.[17] Nonetheless, upstream initiatives have a long-range nature and their benefits are often hard to capture within the usual political cycles, so they are usually subject to the whims of state and provincial politics.

Some have argued that lawmakers have a preference for downstream policies, which can more easily help create local companies and jobs within the timeframe of political cycles.[18] If at the federal level the major concern is with the broad business climate and the environment for innovation, provincial and state governments speak the language of local job creation. Through downstream programs, they are keen to spur and retain new firms within their jurisdictions. Policies to that effect may directly focus on supporting high-tech start-ups, but most often they are part of broader initiatives to stimulate innovation. Not surprisingly then, policy initiatives aimed at entrepreneurship can be found across government departments, agencies, and ministries.[19] A subset of these initiatives directly involves universities, whether as partners or propitious settings for venture creation. In implementing these policies, states and provinces have taken on multiple roles in stimulating entrepreneurship.

A first major role states and provinces have attempted to play is that of financier for new firms. Historically, a large portion of investments in innovative companies in the United States has been centered in the metropolitan regions of San Francisco, Greater Boston, and New York. In the first quarter of 2014, nearly 76 percent of venture capital investments in the United States were concentrated in three states—California, Massachusetts, and New York—and accounted for 62 percent of all venture-backed deals.[20] In Canada, Ontario, Quebéc, and British Columbia also attract the largest amount of venture capital.[21] To ensure university-based entrepreneurs have access to capital, several states have invested in public venture funds, or else partner to create them. In Wisconsin, the government recently established a state-funded pool of venture capital to support companies in high-growth sectors, and in

Vermont, the state's Vermont Seed Capital Fund invests in early stage, technology based companies.[22] Several other states have created venture capital funds that help finance the development of start-up companies specifically aiming to commercialize university research.[23] For instance, the Nevada venture capital program, Battle Born Venture, makes equity investments in early-stage, high-growth enterprises in selected sectors.[24] In Maryland, the state-created Maryland Technology Development Corporation, together with state and local government leaders from Virginia, Delaware and the District of Columbia, launched The Chesapeake Regional Innovation Fund to invest in early-stage companies connected with the region's research laboratories and research universities. In step with the federal government's efforts to bolster the venture capital industry in Canada, provincial governments are promoting funds that finance early stage technology and science companies.[25]

Some states also encourage the creation of expansion of high-growth companies through the use of tax incentives. While some states such as Maine have initiated tax credit programs for investors of start-up and early-stage businesses (e.g., Maine's Seed Capital Tax Credit Program), others have applied tax credits on investments in university-linked start-ups. For example, the State Legislature of Oregon recently introduced a tax credit for financial supporters of university venture development funds at the seven Oregon University System campuses and the Oregon Health & Science University.[26] The New York State Legislature recently passed a law that will create tax-free zones on the institutions of the State University of New York system as well as some campuses of the City University of New York and private colleges in the state. The plan, dubbed StartupNY, is intended to help foster and retain start-up companies, as well as to encourage the expansion of existing companies and to lure out-of-state companies, as long as they are aligned with their host institution's teaching and research missions.[27]

A second role is of inducer of entrepreneurial activity in higher education. These efforts aim to make entrepreneurship important to public universities and colleges, toward greater involvement in supporting student entrepreneurs. In the United States, state governments in Oregon, Florida, and New York have authorized universities and colleges to establish venture development funds for the purpose of facilitating the commercialization of research and to provide incubator facilities to academic entrepreneurs and eligible small businesses.[28] Another effort at encouraging an entrepreneurial culture was taken in the state legislature of Illinois in 2001 when the General Assembly established economic development as the fourth mission of the University of Illinois.[29] Although the resolution supporting the inclusion of economic development as a core mission of state universities emphasized the commercialization of university researchers' inventions, the clear expectation that universities help create jobs and promote a technological economy encouraged the University of Illinois to stimulate student entrepreneurship.[30] Ontario's differentiation framework, discussed below, also seeks to induce some universities to undertake the promotion of entrepreneurship as part of their mission.

A third role is to provide business support for entrepreneurs, involving universities as partners. The well-regarded Ben Franklyn Technology Partners program in Pennsylvania, a pioneer initiative in this area, has for three decades helped small firms partner with universities in the state to address their technology development needs.[31] In Nova Scotia, the Department of Labour and Advanced Education, together with the federal government's Atlantic Canada Opportunities Agency, has funded four new "sandboxes"—collaborative spaces hosted by universities and colleges that will bring together students, mentors and external advisors to take business concepts from idea to execution. Sandbox activities will include a youth entrepreneurship camp, pitch competitions, a speaker series, and a summer accelerator program for high school and university students.[32]

## Policy initiatives since the Great Recession

Unsurprisingly, high-tech entrepreneurship gained prominence in the wake of the Great Recession as a potential solution to the economic slump. In Canada, a number of programs focused on supporting entrepreneurs have been created or expanded, and in the United States new federal initiatives have pushed legislation to facilitate entrepreneurship and supported entrepreneurship infrastructures. These federal initiatives have been implemented through research funding agencies, new special initiatives, and the agencies that promote innovation and entrepreneurship. States and provinces have been active too, seeking to grow start-ups that will contribute to employment generation and economic growth locally. The initiatives of four jurisdictions are discussed to illustrate the roles.

As the United States attempted to recover from the economic depression, the Obama administration established the Office of Innovation and Entrepreneurship within the Department of Commerce's Economic Development Administration (EDA) in October 2009, with a mandate to support entrepreneurs and accelerate the commercialization of federally funded research. This office leads the $15 million 2014 Regional Innovation Strategy Program competition to spur innovation capacity-building activities in regions across the nation.[33] This relatively small program seeks to leverage state and local projects that support early-stage companies, whether through science and research parks or seed capital funds. A more decisive initiative was StartUp America, launched in 2011 as a multipronged White House agenda "to celebrate, inspire, and accelerate high-growth entrepreneurship throughout the nation."[34]

StartUp America contains five policy areas. The first is to increase access to capital among new companies. The second is to connect entrepreneurs with mentors and education. Two initiatives toward this goal are the launching of a national center for teaching innovation and entrepreneurship to support entrepreneurship education at engineering schools throughout the United States, and the Entrepreneurial Mentors Corps program for clean tech start-ups. The third policy area of StartUp America is to reduce barriers to business entry, which includes seed funding through the Small Business Innovation Research (SBIR) program, and allowing entrepreneurs to cap monthly student-loan payments to 10 percent of their income. The fourth is to accelerate innovation: among the related initiatives are the *America Invents Act*, which sought to make patent processing more efficient, and the *America's Next Top Energy Innovator* program which made it easier for start-up companies to license the Department of Energy's unlicensed patents.[35] In addition to these initiatives, the president directed all federal research agencies to streamline and accelerate the process for public–private research partnerships, small business research and development grants, and university-start-up collaborations. The fifth, and final, policy area entails creating market opportunities for innovative entrepreneurs. The bulk of initiatives in this policy area include several open data initiatives. Also emphasized within this policy area is the creation of a national platform for healthcare innovation, which includes fostering engagement among policymakers, entrepreneurs, innovators, and health care professionals.[36]

Also in 2011, the US National Science Foundation (NSF) established the Innovation Corps program (I-Corps) to teach academic researchers how to build profitable start-ups around their technologies.[37] A goal of the I-Corps program is to foster entrepreneurship that will lead to the commercialization of technology arising from NSF-funded research. The program helps to bridge the gap between the research funding provided by NSF and the development of technology credible enough that can raise private capital, or else be license to existing companies. It is also meant to feed the NSF SBIR and Small Business Technology Transfer (STTR) programs, which provide seed capital to early-stage start-ups. In its initial stages, the I-Corps program sent researchers to Stanford University, the University of Michigan, and Georgia Tech for training,[38] but later expanded to include 16 more universities across 12 states. More recently, the NSF awarded grants to consortia of universities in the Bay Area, Maryland-DC, New York, and Los Angeles to act as I-Corps "nodes" to support regional needs for innovation education, infrastructure, and research. According to Errol Arkilic, NSF I-Corps program director, "[t]he nodes are the foundation of a national innovation ecosystem, and focus on the front lines of local and regional commercialization efforts."[39] The National Institutes of Health (NIH) has collaborated with the NSF to develop its own version of the I-Corps program through the NIH Innovation Corps Team Training Pilot Program. This program seeks to accelerate the development of commercialization of new technologies arising from projects supported by researchers already funded by NIH SBIR and STTR awards.[40]

Canada's federal government has taken several steps during this decade to stimulate the creation and growth of innovative companies. Entrepreneurship has also figured prominently in Canada's federal budget plans since the Great Depression. The Economic Action Plan 2012 expanded on previous efforts at promoting entrepreneurs by supporting early-stage risk capital and large-scale venture capital activities. The plan also made permanent the Business-Led Networks of Centres of Excellence program, which funds industry-focused collaborative research networks, and the Canadian Innovation Commercialization Program, which is designed to help entrepreneurs commercialize their innovations. Selected applicants to the program first have their innovations tested by a federal department, and subsequently they are connected with federal procurement activities and potential government users.[41] Support for entrepreneurship became much more direct in Canada's Economic Action Plan 2013. One notable initiative was the Venture Capital Action Plan, a strategy to help increase private sector investments in early-stage risk capital, and to support the creation of large-scale venture capital funds led by the private sector.[42]

The Centres of Excellence for Commercialization and Research program represents a major federal commitment to fostering high-tech ventures. Building upon the long-standing centers of excellence program initiated in the 1980s, which focused on stimulating world class research and university–industry R&D collaboration, this new iteration funds networks and centers across the country with the aim to promote innovation, research commercialization, and entrepreneurship.[43] Among the funded centers are the Canadian Digital Media Network and MaRS Discovery District in Toronto, each of which are connected with university incubators and start-up programs.[44] Another effort at promoting a business ecosystem ripe for entrepreneurs include the Business Innovation Access Program, which connects small- and medium-sized enterprises with universities, colleges, and other research institutions to address and resolve barriers to the commercialization of ideas, products, and services. Introduced in 2014 as part of the Economic Action Plan 2013, the two-year pilot program is managed under IRAP. Eligible projects are those seeking short-term assistance from academic institutions, either for business development (i.e., market research, marketing strategy development) or technical problem-solving (i.e., product or process optimization, specialized testing).[45]

In September 2013, Canada's federal government launched the Canada Accelerator and Incubator Program as part of the Venture Capital Action Plan. The program provided $60 million over a five-year period to nearly a dozen accelerators and incubators, several of which partnering with universities, to expand their services to entrepreneurs. In addition, the Venture Capital Action Plan made available $100 million through the BDC to invest in firms graduating from business accelerators.[46] The BDC was also charged with managing the government's Entrepreneurship Awards, which recognize outstanding Canadian entrepreneurs with the goal of promoting an entrepreneurial culture. The awards are modeled after the BDC's Young Entrepreneur Award, through which the Bank provides funding to promising entrepreneurs aged 18 to 35. Finally, building on its efforts at fostering a culture of entrepreneurship in Canada, the Economic Action Plan 2013 continued government funding of Futurpreneur Canada (formerly the Canadian Youth Business Foundation), a national not-for-profit organization that works with young entrepreneurs through mentorship, expert advice, learning resources, and start-up financing.[47]

High-tech entrepreneurs have been at the forefront of immigration debates as well. Some have argued that the United States, historically a hotbed of opportunity for entrepreneurial talent, is quickly losing terrain. Obtrusive immigration policies and competition from countries with friendlier regulations and incentives contribute to making the United States less attractive to prospective immigrants and foreign entrepreneurs already in the country.[48] In Canada, the Start-Up Visa Program already encourages foreign entrepreneurs to immigrate. Non-Canadians with a business venture or idea supported by a designated venture capital fund, angel investor group, or business incubator, and with at least one year of postsecondary education, sufficient settlement funds, and knowledge of English or French are eligible to apply. The program is credited with attracting entrepreneurs who would have struggled to immigrate to, or stay in the United States under that country's current immigration system.[49] In 2014, President Obama issued an executive order on immigration that introduced measures to increase the immigration options available for foreign entrepreneurs.[50]

To specifically support university students engage in entrepreneurship, loan deference and forbearance options are also being implemented. The US SBA Income-Based Repayment Plan supports recent college graduates who are looking to start a business or join a start-up by deferring federal student loans.[51] In Ontario, supporting entrepreneurs was key part of the 2013 provincial budget. Recognizing the need to help young people start companies and create jobs, the government funded a comprehensive Youth Jobs Strategy.[52]

States and provinces have also renewed and initiated efforts with universities to spur start-up activity. The jurisdictions below have comparable economies, and have since the Great Recession involved universities in their efforts to stimulate their regional economies.[53] Their policy efforts illustrate the range of approaches currently employed at the state and provincial level to spur high-tech entrepreneurship.

## British Columbia

British Columbia has a history of being a natural resource-based economy, centered on the forestry industry and mining. Today, the province has a diversified economy, with services-producing industries accounting for three-fourths of GDP.⁵⁴ Over the last decade, British Columbia has typically had the largest percentage of the working population involved in start-ups in Canada.⁵⁵ Nonetheless, the province was behind Alberta and Ontario in the share of highly educated entrepreneurs in 2013. Most entrepreneurial activity is concentrated in Vancouver, the province's largest and most dynamic city. The city is home to the province's largest research universities, and is an increasingly important center for software development, biotechnology, aerospace, video game development, and television and film production.

The provincial government has invested in high-tech entrepreneurship through the British Columbia Innovation Council (BCIC), the main provincial agency promoting innovation. BCIC runs a range of upstream and downstream programs, supporting from research chairs in key technological sectors in the province's universities, to a network of business accelerators around the province. Entrepreneurship figures prominently among the council's priorities, as a key component of the provincial government's job generation agenda.⁵⁶ BCIC has partnered with several public and private organizations to implement its initiatives, including the province's universities.

To fulfill its mission of fostering entrepreneurship, the BCIC established the Acceleration Network, which sponsors a venture growth program for technology entrepreneurs at accelerators from across the province.⁵⁷ BCIC is also the lead partner of a technology business idea competition, the BCIC-New Venture Competition. The competition provides training to entrepreneurs during a ten-week seminar and networking series, during which participants compete to win prizes. Among the partners supporting this competition are provincial universities. Finally, BCIC supports Launch Academy, a nonprofit organization that helps entrepreneurs and start-ups learn how to build technology companies.

Together with the Alacrity Foundation—an institution devoted to advancing entrepreneurship, business, and management education in the technology sector—BCIC supported the creation of business incubators in which teams of postsecondary engineering and business students, as well as recent graduates, work on product development and commercialization projects related to ICT. Upon completion of the program, student teams that develop products with market potential are incorporated into jointly owned companies. Those companies can access financial support provided by Wesley Clover International Corporation, an investment management firm and holding company. An agreement between the Alacrity Foundation and the University of Victoria, and supported by BCIC and Wesley Clover, enables engineering graduate students at the university to apply to the program, during which they work on an accelerated schedule to earn their Masters of Applied Science degree while also obtaining a Business Diploma.[58]

The BCIC currently directly supports entrepreneurship at universities through the "entrepreneurship@initative." At the University of British Columbia (UBC), the entrepreneurship@UBC Accelerator Program supports the development of UBC-linked ventures. Moreover, the BCIC was a founding partner in establishing the initial capitalization for the e@UBC Seed Accelerator Fund. At the nearby University of Simon Fraser, the technology entrepreneurship@SFU program joins third- and fourth-year business and applied science students to develop technological products. Students receive entrepreneurship training, guidance, and mentorship in developing an idea before having the opportunity to participate in a pitch competition. The competition winners are funded to turn their ideas and prototypes into businesses. In addition, the BCIC previously contributed to the SFU Venture Connection Program, a university-wide program that supports students exploring entrepreneurship and provides business development support.

In addition to the BCIC, other government bodies support entrepreneurship in the province. This support is typically oriented toward social causes. The BC Government is a sponsor of the Forum for Women Entrepreneurs, which supports and mentors women who are venturing into new business opportunities or ready to grow their existing business. The provincial government has also provided financial support to the Women's Enterprise Centre, which was established by the Western Economic Diversification Canada (a department of the Government of Canada).[59] The Ministry of Aboriginal Relations and Reconciliation and Human Resources and Skills Development Canada supports the Aboriginal Business and Entrepreneurship Skills Training program to assist participants identify business opportunities, determine their feasibility, and design business plan.[60] In 2014, the City of Vancouver, in collaboration with the Vancouver Economic Commission (VEC) and the Vancity Community Foundation, announced plans to open a Technology and Social Innovation Centre to support entrepreneurs, social innovators, and nonprofit organizations through incubation and acceleration programming.[61]

## Indiana

Indiana has the highest concentration of private sector manufacturing jobs in the nation, and manufacturing contributes more to Indiana's economy than it does across all other states.[62] As might be expected, Indianapolis—the most populous city in the state, and the twelfth largest city in the country—has a lower proportion of manufacturing jobs than the rest of the state, and a higher concentration of jobs in professional, scientific, and technical services. Transportation equipment and the life science industries (pharmaceuticals and medical instruments) are the leading export industries in Indiana. The pharmaceutical industry is especially large, ranking fourth among all US states in total sales of pharmaceutical products.[63] Nevertheless, the state has one of the lowest entrepreneurial activity rates and ranks 44th nationally in the percent of employment accounted for by young firms.[64]

In 2011, the state legislature required the Indiana Economic Development Corporation to establish a program to promote the business proposals of students in entrepreneurial programs at state educational institutions. Despite relatively low levels of entrepreneurial activity in the state, entrepreneurship programs at Ball State University and Indiana University are both well recognized,[65] while Purdue University maintains a network of nationally recognized technology-based incubators.[66] Through the resulting Young Entrepreneurs Program the Indiana Small Business Development Center works with local and regional communities to provide incentives to the college-aged entrepreneurs to launch their business venture within their local communities.[67] Participants are required to submit business plans to the Small Business Development Center for consideration in the program. Once approved, participants have an opportunity to attend a pre-event workshop in their area where community leaders and business professors provide coaching and feedback.[68]

The state formed Elevate Ventures in 2011 as a nonprofit organization to directly support emerging start-ups with investor and venture capital. Start-up capital sources from state and federal program are distributed into funds intended to support entrepreneurs in the life sciences, information technology, and advanced manufacturing industries.[69] In addition to assisting local entrepreneurs with its own resources, Elevate Ventures has created the Northeast Indiana Investor Network to connect Northeast Indiana investors with early-stage start-ups. The Indiana Angel Network works with Elevate Ventures and the Northeast Indiana Regional Partnership to help identify and fund companies within Northeast Indiana.[70]

Advancing innovation in the state of Indiana is a key policy issue for Governor Mike Pence. Soon after becoming governor in 2013, Governor Pence declared, "the season of the entrepreneur has begun," and led a handful of initiatives to support innovation and entrepreneurship, including lowering business taxes, allowing entrepreneurs to raise capital through crowdfunding, and forming the Indiana Biosciences Research Institute to accelerate innovation and commercialization in the life sciences.[71] In 2013, Governor Pence signed Executive Order 13–17 to establish the Office of Small Business and Entrepreneurship (OSBE) to align state efforts in supporting entrepreneurship and small business expansion.[72] One core activity of the center is to link university, government, and private sector entrepreneurship programs. The OSBE operates the ten Indiana Small Business Development Centers that support small businesses by providing entrepreneurs expert with business assistance and access to resources. Funding for the regional centers comes from a range of public and private organizations including state universities.[73] In 2014, the Indiana Small Business Development Center partnered with Launch Fishers (a public–private business incubator in Fishers, Indiana) to establish Launch Indiana. Launch Indiana will connect entrepreneurs with mentorship, education, and assistance from successful entrepreneurs.[74]

The OSBE has also partnered with TechPoint, Indiana's statewide technology growth initiative, to launch Tailwind, an initiative aimed at growing Indiana's most promising start-ups. The new initiative aims to increase entrepreneurial education, start-up promotion, and investment to help technology start-ups accelerate their growth. With its IndyX initiative, TechPoint is partnering with companies, universities, and business associations to attract and retain skilled individuals by connecting them with Indianapolis technology companies. The initiative offers summer internships to students in the state, as well as recruitment events to attract technology professionals to Indianapolis. Several of the city's influential technology companies, the Indiana Economic Development

Corporation and Lilly Endowment have helped to finance and support the initiative.[75] Furthermore, TechPoint connects entrepreneurs with venture capital and hosts Entrepreneur Bootcamps to which it provides start-ups with information on critical topics including fundraising, product development, staffing, and investor relations. Finally, TechPoint supports the Governor Bob Orr Indiana Entrepreneurial Fellowship, which places graduates of Indiana universities and colleges with firms in the Indianapolis area. The purpose of the initiative is to provide training, mentorship, and networking for future entrepreneurs and business leaders, with the overarching aim of retaining them in state. During their two-year tenure as Orr Fellows, recent college graduates work at a host company while participating in a variety of events, such as monthly meetings to learn from guest speakers and a ten-week entrepreneurship class.[76]

# Ontario

Ontario is Canada's leading manufacturing province, with southern Ontario being the largest industrialized area in the country. Like the American manufacturing regions just south of its border, many communities in Ontario have experienced the dislocation of old manufacturing plants and challenges to promoting economic renewal. Since the 1980s, the provincial government has supported the development of knowledge-intensive business sectors.[77] In the last few years, this emphasis has included support for entrepreneurship.

The provincial government directly supports several entrepreneurship and innovation centers. The government formed in 2009 the Ontario Network of Excellence designed to help entrepreneurs, businesses, and researchers across the province commercialize their ideas. In 2013, the program was renamed the Ontario Network of Entrepreneurs, signaling the increasing prominence of entrepreneurship in innovation support initiatives. The network consists largely of provincial colleges and venture incubators/accelerators.[78] The incubators and accelerators part of the network receive funding from the ONE, and typically receive support from local municipalities and even the federal government. For instance, the Accelerator Centre in the city of Stratford receives funding from Federal and Provincial Governments, Ontario Centres of Excellence, the Regional Municipality of Waterloo, the City of Waterloo, and the

University of Waterloo, along with industry and academic partners.[79] The network is under the Ontario Centers of Excellence.

Supporting entrepreneurs was key part of 2013 provincial budget. Recognizing the need to help young people start companies and create jobs, the government funded a comprehensive Youth Jobs Strategy.[80] As part of the strategy, the provincial government created the Campus Linked Accelerators program, with an investment of $20 million in accelerators based in the province's universities and colleges. In all, ten venture accelerator programs were funded. Through the strategy, the provincial government also provided $5 million to establish and fund the On-Campus Entrepreneurship Activities program, which is intended to create focal points on university and college campuses for entrepreneurship, and to expose students to the principles of entrepreneurship. For both initiatives, funded universities or colleges are expected to partner with regional innovation centers and local entrepreneurship communities.[81] As part of the suite of programs for promoting entrepreneurship under Ontario's Youth Jobs Strategy, the provincial government is also making $9 million available for the SmartStart Seed Fund, which provides funding for entrepreneurship skills training and seed financing to help student entrepreneurs grow their companies. The Youth Job Strategy also created Entrepreneurship Fellowships to support postsecondary students build start-ups within key sectors. All of the above initiatives are managed by the Ontario Centres of Excellence, which is tasked with fostering innovation and entrepreneurship in the province.[82]

The provincial government also supports a number of entrepreneurship programs that aimed 18 to 29 year olds.[83] Starter Company, Summery Company, and Strategic Community Entrepreneurship Projects are three of such programs that provide training, support, and small funding to young entrepreneurs. In addition, the province funded the Youth Business Acceleration Program with $7 million to offer entrepreneurship education, market research services, and mentorship to entrepreneurs in this age group. The Youth Investment Accelerator Fund invests up to $500,000 in technology-based start-ups that have graduated from a recognized accelerator program within the province—many of those are based in universities. Both programs are managed by the MaRS Discovery District—an organization dedicated to commercializing research from Toronto's top universities, medical institutions, and research institutes.[84] The programs are delivered through a network of partners that are part of the Ontario Network of Entrepreneurs.

In addition, the province has taken a step toward creating incentives for higher education institutions in the province that excel in supporting entrepreneurship to make it a distinctive area of focus. Ontario's Differentiation Policy Framework for Postsecondary Education reinforced the importance of entrepreneurial activity as a component used to evaluate colleges and universities, and suggested it as a means by which some campuses may distinguish themselves from others.[85]

# Illinois

Illinois is one of the most productive manufacturing states, and home to many of the largest companies in the United States.[86] The business center of the state is Chicago, the state's most populated city, and also among the largest and wealthiest city in the country. From 2006 to 2011, the state of Illinois has had twice the national average of companies funded by venture capital. In 2012, Chicago was ranked fifth Metropolitan Statistical Area for new business established, and there has been 23 percent annual growth in start-up creation since 2010. Since then, over 280 university-affiliated start-ups have been created, and an average of 20 university technology spin-off companies have been formed every year. Moreover, a reported 80 percent of university start-ups remain in Illinois.[87]

In 2011, the state government created the Illinois Innovation Council to identify and advance strategies to accelerate innovation, economic growth, and job creation in the state.[88] The first initiative of the Innovation Council was the formation of the Illinois Innovation Network, an online platform to connect start-ups, innovation-driven enterprises, service providers, research and academic institutions, and community leaders.[89] Another project is the Illinois Corporate-Startup Challenge. Launched in 2013, the Challenge recruits corporations biannually and works to identify their innovation needs. Start-ups are referred to the program by universities, venture capital firms, incubator, and nonprofit groups throughout the state. A number of start-ups are chosen to pitch at private demo days, potentially resulting in business contracts, investments, mentorship opportunities, and more. The Illinois Innovation Council's programs are managed by the Illinois Science & Technology Coalition, a member-driven nonprofit organization intent on fostering technology-based economic development.

The Chicago Mayor Rahm Emanuel chairs World Business Chicago, a public–private partnership between the City and its business community concerned with economic development. WBC is also home to the ChicagoNEXT council of technology leaders, a dedicated effort to drive business growth and opportunity in science, innovation, and technology entrepreneurship.[90] 1871, a digital-technology start-up incubator in Chicago, was launched in May 2012 by a nonprofit organization, with $2.3 million in seed funding from the state government. Northwestern University, University of Chicago, University of Illinois, Illinois Institute of Technology, and DeVry Education Group all have dedicated spaces at 1871 where students and faculty come to work on their businesses and immerse themselves in Chicago's entrepreneurial community. In June 2014, the state pledged a $2.5 million grant and $1.5 million loan to build a second start-up incubator adjacent to 1871 that will support entrepreneurship in medical and biotechnology fields.[91] These join the University of Illinois's new incubator for life-sciences start-ups, which was established in 2013 with matched funds from the state.[92]

Like many states, Illinois has organizations devoted to supporting small businesses. The Illinois Small Business Development Center (SBDC) Network provides business advice and management assistance to small businesses, and is funded in part through a cooperative agreement with the US Small Business Administration. Since 2011, SBDCs have offered services to help entrepreneurs commercialize new ideas into innovative products, services, and business models. These programs are funded through the Illinois Department of Commerce and Economic Opportunity, with matching funds from sponsoring SBDC host organizations.[93] Most are located on university of college campuses.

In an example of university–government–private partnership to stimulate entrepreneurship, the University of Wisconsin, Whitewater spearheaded the State of Ingenuity Initiative. The initiative is a regional collaboration of educational institutions, economic development organizations, and business incubators that supports accelerators and other organizations that assist start-ups. The initiative coordinates efforts to support entrepreneurs across the six-county region of northern Illinois and southeastern Wisconsin. The collaboration, funded by a grant from the Economic Development Administration in 2010, is aimed at driving economic renewal for a mostly rural region impacted by auto plant closures and major job layoffs.[94]

\* \* \*

The federal governments of the United States and Canada have taken on supporting entrepreneurial activity through various means; special legislative initiatives, dedicated programs focused on harnessing innovation through start-ups, and new funding schemes through research funding agencies have all been used. These initiatives follow from national science, technology, and innovation agendas, and harbour expectations for remediating competitiveness challenges and underemployment. At the state and provincial level, universities have come to the forefront over the last few decades in policies supporting high-tech entrepreneurship. State and provincial governments have responsibility over higher education, and preparing and supporting future entrepreneurs has become part of the expectations of policymakers regarding public universities.

Public support for entrepreneurs is not without criticism. Some opponents claim that such initiatives will orient universities and colleges toward "corporatization"—the replacement of academic values by a commercial mindset oriented toward profit generation.[95] Others question the desirability of start-ups as a vehicle for job creation. They argue that jobs in small firms tend to exist for a shorter period of time, pay lower wages, and have less generous fringe benefits than jobs created by large firms.[96] Indeed, entrepreneurship expert Scott Share points out that the typical start-up is less innovative and productive than more mature firms, and many create few jobs and little wealth.[97] Moreover, critics point to poorer working conditions, less job training, and higher job turnover rates in small companies. Another set of critiques focuses on the forms of government policy support to encourage entrepreneurship and their consequences. Some argue that government programs risk over-investing in start-ups, with one consequence being the subsiding of entrepreneurs and their business ventures that nevertheless fail.[98] Others assert that policies could have unintended effects of diverting entrepreneurial efforts into bidding for subsidies.[99] Questions also remain about the usual policy tools employed to support entrepreneurs. For instance, the effectiveness of tax credits as incentives for firm creation is unclear, since neophyte companies do not typically generate taxable profit in their early years.[100] One critic counters the growing faith in entrepreneurship by arguing that policymakers pose inordinate faith in entrepreneurs and their ability to commercially exploit scientific research.[101]

Notwithstanding these criticisms, the allure of technology entrepreneurs has remained unabated through the 2010s. Supporting the creation of innovative start-ups is a standard recipe for state and provincial governments, economic development agencies, and university administrators. In this climate, policy initiatives have been a powerful driver of the entrepreneurship movement in universities. General support for the kinds of policies examined above has remained stable, despite the open questions on the effectiveness of certain policy instruments. As illustrated in the cases examined in this chapter, universities have been central to their implementation, whether as partners in initiatives to support entrepreneurs or as settings where start-ups served by government programs are established.

## Notes

1 Erika Fitzpatrick, *Innovation America: A Final Report* (National Governors Association, Washington DC: 2007); National Governors Association, *Innovation America: Investing in Innovation* (Washington DC: National Governors Association, Pew Center on the States, 2007).
2 Glen Hodgson, *Building an Innovative Nation one Entrepreneur at a Time: BDC 2010 Legislative Review* (The Business Development Bank of Canada, Ottawa, Industry Canada, 2011).
3 "History," America's Small *Business Development Centers (SBDC)*, accessed October 4, 2014, http://americassbdc.org/about-us/history/.
4 "About Office of Entrepreneurship Education," *U.S. Small Business Administration*, accessed October 4, 2014, https://www.sba.gov/offices/headquarters/oee/about-us.
5 Donald Fisher, Kjell Rubenson, Jean Bernatchez, Robert Clift, Glen Jones, Jacy Lee, Madeleine MacIvor, John Meredith, Theresa Shanahan, and Claude Trottier, *Canadian Federal Policy and Postsecondary Education* (Vancouver: Centre for Policy Studies in Higher Education and Training, Faculty of Education, University of British Columbia, 2006).
6 Erik R. Pages, Doris Freedman, and Patrick Von Bargen, "Entrepreneurship as a State and Local Economic Development Strategy," in *The Emergence of Entrepreneurship Policy: Governance, Start-ups, and growth in the US Knowledge Economy*, ed. David M. Hart (Cambridge: Cambridge University Press, 2003), 240–259.
7 David B. Audretsch and Iris Beckmann, "From Small Business to Entrepreneurship Policy," in *The Handbook of Research on Entrepreneurship Policy*, eds. David B. Audretsch, Isabel Grilo, and A. Roy Thurik (Cheltenham, UK: Edward Elgar Publishing, 2007), 51.
8 David B. Audretsch, Isabel Grilo, and A. Roy Thurik, eds., *The Handbook of Research on Entrepreneurship Policy* (Cheltenham, UK: Edward Elgar Publishing, 2007).

9   Ibid.
10  C. Stewart Gillmore, *Fred Terman at Stanford: Building a Discipline, a University, and Silicon Valley* (Stanford: Stanford University Press, 2004).
11  See, for instance, Stuart W. Leslie and Robert H. Kargon, "Selling Silicon Valley: Frederick Terman's Model for Regional Advantage," *Business History Review*, 70, no. 4 (1996): 435–472.
12  Roger L. Geiger, *Knowledge and Money: Research Universities and the Paradox of the Marketplace* (Stanford: Stanford University Press, 2004); Allison Bramwell and David A. Wolfe, "Universities and Regional Economic Development: The Entrepreneurial University of Waterloo," *Research Policy* 37, no. 8 (2008): 1175–1187.
13  Dan Berglund and Christopher Coburn, *Partnerships: A Compendium of State and Federal Cooperative Technology Programs* (Columbus, OH: Battelle Press, 1995); Peter K. Eisinger, *The Rise of the Entrepreneurial State: State and Local Economic Development Policy in the United States* (Madison, WI: University of Wisconsin Press, 1988); Peter K. Eisinger, "State Economic Development in the 1990s: Politics and Policy Learning," *Economic Development Quarterly* 9 (1995): 146–158; Walter H. Plosila, "State Science and Technology-Based Economic Development Policy: History, Trends and Developments and Future Directions," *Economic Development Quarterly* 18, no. 2 (2004): 113–126.
14  Roger L. Geiger and Creso Sá, "Beyond Technology Transfer: U.S. State Policies to Harness University Research for Economic Development," *Minerva* 43, no. 1 (2005): 1–21; E. J. Douglas, "Entrepreneurship and Management Education: A Case for Change." *Journal of Management and Entrepreneurship* 1, no. 2 (2006): 1–17.
15  Creso Sá, "Redefining University Roles in Regional Economies: A Case Study of University-Industry Relations and Academic Organization in Nanotechnology," *Higher Education: The International Journal of Higher Education and Educational Planning* 61, no. 2 (2011): 193–208.
16  Irwin Feller, "American State Governments as Models for National Science Policy," *Journal of Policy Analysis and Management* 11, no. 2 (1992): 288–309; Maryann P. Feldman, Lauren Lanahan, and Iryna Lendel, "Experiments in the Laboratories of Democracy: State Scientific Capacity Building," *Economic Development Quarterly* 28, no. 2 (2014): 107–131.
17  Roger Geiger and Creso Sá. *Tapping the Riches of Science: Universities and the Promise of Economic Growth* (Cambridge, MA: Harvard University Press, 2009).
18  Feller, "American State Governments as Models for National Science Policy."
19  Lois A. Stevenson and Andres Lundstrom, *Entrepreneurship Policy: Theory and Practice* (New York: Springer, 2005).
20  "VC Investments Q1 '14—MoneyTree—National Data," *National Venture Capital Association*, accessed September 2, 2014, http://www.nvca.org/index.php?option=com_docman&task=cat_view&gid=57&Itemid=317.

21. "SME Research and Statistics: Q4 2013," *Industry Canada*, last modified May 28, 2014, http://www.ic.gc.ca/eic/site/061.nsf/eng/h_02881.html.
22. *Trends in Tech-Based Economic Development: Local, State, and Federal Action in 2013* (Westervile, OH: State Science & Technology Institute, 2014), accessed March 5, 2014, http://ssti.org/report-archive/trends2013.pdf.
23. Michael N. Bastedo and Nathan F. Harris, "The State Role in Entrepreneurship and Economic Development: Governance, Oversight, and Public University Start-up Innovation," in ed. Gary D. Libecap, *Measuring the Social Value of Innovation: A Link in the University Technology Transfer and Entrepreneurship Equation* (Bingley, UK: Emerald, 2009), 215–235; *Trends in Tech-Based Economic Development: Local, State, and Federal Action in 2012* (Westervile, OH: State Science & Technology Institute, 2013), accessed March 5, 2014, http://ssti.org/sites/default/files/trends2012.pdf.
24. *Battle Born Venture: Nevada's State Venture Capital Program*, accessed October 14, 2014, http://battlebornventure.com.
25. For examples, see "Alberta Enterprise announces $10 million investment in Accelerate Fund LP," *Accelerate Fund* (November 14, 2012), http://www.acceleratefund.ca/news-2/; "Provincial Government Provides $20 Million to Drive Entrepreneurial Success," *Government of Newfoundland and Labrador* (November 4, 2014), accessed December 4, 2014, http://www.releases.gov.nl.ca/releases/2014/exec/1104n02.aspx; Matthew Kang, "Ontario Premier Launches $300M Venture Capital Fund in Kitchener, *CBC.ca* (January 21, 2014), accessed March 8, 2014, http://www.cbc.ca/news/canada/kitchener-waterloo/ontario-premier-launches-300m-venture-capital-fund-in-kitchener-1.2505447.
26. "Oregon Tax Credit," University Venture Development Fund, University of Oregon, accessed on October 5, 2014, http://www.uoventurefund.uoregon.edu/taxcredit/index.html.
27. Start-Up NY, accessed November 2, http://startup.ny.gov.
28. *Trends in Tech-Based Economic Development: Local, State, and Federal Action in 2013* (State Science & Technology Institute, 2014).
29. University of Illinois at Urbana-Champaign, *Transforming a Larger, Complex Research University into a More Entrepreneurial Organization: The University of Illinois at Urbana-Champaign in Collaboration with the Ewing Marion Kauffman Foundation* (Kansas City, KS: Kauffman Foundation, 2012).
30. Ibid.
31. Geiger and Sá, "Beyond Technology Transfer."
32. Premier's Office, "Sandboxes Encourage Innovation, Entrepreneurship (March 19, 2014), accessed October 5, 2014, http://novascotia.ca/news/release/?id=20140319003.
33. "U.S. Department of Commerce Announces $15 Million Grant Competition to Spur Regional Innovation," *U.S. Economic Development Administration* (September 4, 2014), accessed October 6, 2014, http://www.eda.gov/news/press-releases/2014/09/04/regional-innovat ion-grant.htm.

34 "Startup America," *The White House*, accessed November 23, 2014, http://www.whitehouse.gov/economy/business/startup-america.

35 *Leahy-Smith America Invents Act*, HR 1249, 112th Cong., 1st sess., *Congressional Record* 157, no. 132 (September 8, 2011), S5402–S5442; "America's Next Top Energy Innovator Challenge," *U.S. Department of Energy*, accessed November 2, 2014, http://energy.gov/science-innovation/innovation/americas-next-top-energy-innovator/americas-next-top-energy-innovator.

36 One step in this direction was the creation of the Investing in Innovation (i2) Initiative under the Office of the National Coordinator for Health Information Technology. The i2 Initiative awards prizes and hosts venture competitions to accelerate the development of solutions to key challenges in health IT. See "Health IT Prizes & Challenges," *Office of the National Coordinator for Health Information Technology*, last updated January 15, 2013, http://www.healthit.gov/policy-researchers-implementers/health-it-prizes-challenges.

37 "I-Corps: To Strengthen the Impact of Scientific Discoveries," *National Science Foundation* (press release 11–153), July 28, 2011, accessed March 17, 2014, http://www.nsf.gov/news/news_summ.jsp?cntn_id=121225.

38 Wade Roush, "National Science Foundation Scales Up Entrepreneurship Program," *Xconomy*, February 21, 2013, accessed November 30, 2014, http://www.xconomy.com/san-francisco/2013/02/21/national-science-foundation-scales-up-entrepreneurship-program/.

39 "New Grants to Innovation Corps 'Nodes' Further Enhance Public-Private Partnership" *National Science Foundation* (press release 13–028), February 21, 2013, accessed October 2, 2014, http://www.nsf.gov/news/news_summ.jsp?cntn_id=127011.

40 "PAR-14-261: Innovation Corps (I-Corps) Team Training Pilot Program for NIH Phase 1 Small Business Innovation Research (SBIR) and Small Business Technology Transfer (STTR) Grantees," *National Institutes of Health*, accessed November 10, 2014, http://grants.nih.gov/grants/guide/pa-files/PAR-14-261.html.

41 "Canadian Innovation Commercialization Program," *Canada's Economic Action Plan, Government of Canada,* accessed November 23, 2014, http://actionplan.gc.ca/en/initiative/canadian-innovation-commercialization-program.

42 "Venture Capital Action Plan," *Canada's Economic Action Plan, Government of Canada,* accessed November 23, 2014, http://actionplan.gc.ca/en/initiative/venture-capital-action-plan-0.

43 For the development of the centres of excellence, see Atkinson Grosjean, *Public Science, Private Interests: Culture and Commerce in Canada's Networks of Centres of Excellence* (Montreal: McGill-Queen's University Press, 2006).

44 "Centres of Excellence for Commercialization and Research," *Networks of Centres of Excellence of Canada,* accessed on November 8, 2014, http://www.nce-rce.gc.ca/NetworksCentres-CentresReseaux/CECR-CECR_eng.asp.

45. "Business Innovation Access Program" *National Research Council of Canada*, accessed November 23, 2014, http://www.nrc-cnrc.gc.ca/eng/irap/biap/.
46. "Innovation Hubs That Foster Entrepreneurial Talent and Ideas," *Canada's Economic Action Plan*, accessed October 3, 2014, http://actionplan.gc.ca/en/initiative/innovation-hubs-foster-entrepreneurial-talent-and.
47. "Canada Youth Business Foundation," *Canada's Economic Action Plan, Government of Canada*, accessed November 23, 2014, http://actionplan.gc.ca/en/initiative/canada-youth-business-foundation.
48. Vivek Wadhwa, *The Immigrant Exodus: Why America Is Losing the Global Rage to Capture Entrepreneurial Talent* (Philadelphia, PA: Wharton Digital Press, 2012).
49. Brenda Bouw, "Visa Program Opens Doors to Overseas Talent," *The Global and Mail*, October 15, 2014, accessed October 15, 2014 http://www.theglobeandmail.com/report-on-business/small-business/starting-out/visa-program-opens-doors-to-overseas-talent/article21087842/.
50. "Fact Sheet: Immigration Accountability Executive Action," *The White House*, November 20, 2014, accessed December 1, 2014, http://www.whitehouse.gov/the-press-office/2014/11/20/fact-sheet-immigration-accountability-executive-action.
51. "Student Start-Up Plan America," *U.S. Small Business Administration*, accessed November 10, 2014, https://www.sba.gov/startupamerica/student-startup-plan.
52. "Jobs and Opportunity for Youth: New Ontario Government Plans to Tackle Youth Unemployment," *Government of Ontario, Office of the Premier* (news release) April 29, 2013, accessed November 12, 2014, http://www.tcu.gov.on.ca/eng/document/nr/13.07/bg0729.html.
53. Ontario and Illinois are similar in population size (12,581,821 and 12,882,135 respectively) and in GDP per capita (US$41,404 and 37,855), while Indiana has a larger population than British Columbia (6,570,902 and 4,400,057) but a slightly smaller GDP per capita (US$ 37,855 and 38,411). In US dollars (January 2015). Sources: Statistics Canada, US Census, US Bureau of Economic Analysis.
54. *2013 British Columbia Financial and Economic Review, 73rd Edition* (British Columbia: Ministry of Finance, August 2013).
55. *BDC index of new entrepreneurial activity 2012* (Business Development Bank of Canada, 2012).
56. "Canada Starts Here," *BC Jobs Plan, Government of British Columbia*, accessed November 10, 2014, http://engage.gov.bc.ca/bcjobsplan/.
57. "BC Venture Acceleration Program," *BC Innovation Council*, accessed November 10, 2014, http://www.bcacceleration.ca.
58. "Programs and Initiatives," *BC Innovation Council*, accessed November 9, 2014, http://www.bcic.ca/programs/entrepreneurshipuvic.
59. "Harper Government Supports Professional and Entrepreneurial Women in British Columbia," *Status of Women Canada, Government of Canada* (news

release) December 16, 2014, accessed December 20, 2014, http://www.swc-cfc.gc.ca/med/news-nouvelles/2014/1216-eng.html.

60 "BEST—Aboriginal Business and Entrepreneurship Skills Training," Government of British Columbia, accessed November 20, 2014, http://www.gov.bc.ca/arr/economic/fcf/strategy.html.

61 "City and Partners Announce Plan to Open Technology and Social Innovation Centre," *City of Vancouver*, October 3, 2014, accessed November 7, 2014, http://vancouver.ca/news-calendar/city-and-partners-announce-plan-to-open-technology-social-innovation-centre.aspx.

62 Maureen GroppeGannett, "Indiana Economy Grew Faster Than Nation's," *The Indianapolis Star*, August 25, 2014, accessed November 20, 2014, http://www.indystar.com/story/news/2014/08/25/indiana-economy-grew-faster-nations/14553073/.

63 Matt R. Kinghorn and Timothy F. Slaper, *The Indiana Life Science Industries* (Indiana Business Research Center for the Indiana Economic Development Corporation, Bloomington, IN, April 2009).

64 "Business Dynamics Statistics Briefing: Entrepreneurship across States," *Kauffman Foundation*, February 2009, accessed November 23, 2014, http://www.kauffman.org/what-we-do/research/business-dynamics-statistics/business-dynamics-statistics-briefing-entrepreneurship-across-states; Robert W. Fairlie, *Kauffman Index of Entrepreneurial Activity 1996–2013* (Kansas City, MO: Kauffman Foundation, 2013).

65 "List of Rankings and Recognitions Highlights," *Ball State University*, accessed November 4, 2014, http://cms.bsu.edu/academics/centersandinstitutes/entrepreneurshipcenter/rankingsandrecognitions/listofrankingsandrecognitionshighlights; "Entrepreneurship Rankings," *U.S. News and World Report*, last updated September 9, 2014, http://colleges.usnews.rankingsandreviews.com/best-colleges/rankings/business-entrepreneurship.

66 "AURP Annual Award Recipients: Outstanding Research/Science Park Achievement Award," *Association of University Research Parks*, accessed November 20, 2014, http://web.archive.org/web/20080112195707/http://www.aurp.net/more/awards.cfm.

67 In running the Young Entrepreneurs Program, the Indiana Small Business Development Centers work in partnership with the state's Office of Community and Rural Affairs and the Indiana Economic Development Corporation.

68 "Young Entrepreneurs Program," *Indiana Small Business Development Center*, accessed November 8, 2014, http://isbdc.org/yep/.

69 "We Help By: Providing Startup Capital & Funding to Entrepreneurs," *Elevate Ventures*, accessed November 8, 2014, http://www.elevateventures.com/programs/indiana-venture-capital-funding.

70 *Indiana Angel Network*, accessed November 30, 2014, http://www.indianaangelnetwork.com.

71  Mike Pence, "'Season of the Entrepreneur' Dawns in Hoosier State: Indiana Governor," *CNBC.com*, June 18, 2014, accessed October 24, 2014, http://www.cnbc.com/id/101769713#.
72  "Statewide Partners," *Indiana Small Business Development Center*, accessed November 8, 2014, http://isbdc.org/partners/.
73  "About Us," *Indiana Small Business Development Center*, accessed November 8, 2014, http://isbdc.org/about-us/.
74  Erik Scheub, "ISBDC Partners with Launch Fishers to Create Launch Indiana SBDC," *Indiana Business Development Center*, January 22, 2014, accessed January 22, 2014, http://isbdc.org/isbdc-partners-with-launch-fishers-to-create-launch-indiana-sbdc/.
75  Joshua Hall, "IndyX: TechPoint Pilots Talent Attraction and Retention Initiative for Tech Sector," *TechPoint*, November 26, 2013, accessed November 26, 2014, http://techpoint.org/indyx-techpoint-pilots-talent-attraction-and-retention-initiative-for-tech-sector/.
76  Kate Dowrey, "Be the Yes Person," *Orr Entrepreneurial Fellowship*, December 12, 2014, accessed December 13, 2014, http://blog.orrfellowship.org/blog/kate-dowrey/be-the-yes-person.
77  Creso Sá, "Canadian Provinces and Public Policies for University Research," *Higher Education Policy* 23 (2010): 335–357.
78  "About Us," *Ontario Centres of Excellence*, accessed November 30, 2014, http://www.oce-ontario.org/about-us/the-one.
79  "Partners," *The Accelerator Centre*, accessed November 30, 2014, http://acceleratorcentre.com/about/partners/.
80  "New and Enhanced Programs to Assist Student Entrepreneurs Now Rolling Out across the Province," *Ontario Centres of Excellence*, September 25, 2014, accessed October 1, 2014, http://www.oce-ontario.org/news-events/news/news-archives/2014/09/25/new-and-enhanced-programs-to-assist-student-entrepreneurs-now-rolling-out-across-the-province.
81  "On-Campus Entrepreneurship Activities Program," *Ontario Centres of Excellence*, accessed on October 11, 2014, http://www.oce-ontario.org/docs/default-source/default-document-library/at-a-glance---ocea.pdf?sfvrsn=2.
82  "Entrepreneurship Programs," *Ontario Centres of Excellence*, accessed on October 11, 2014, http://www.oce-ontario.org/programs/entrepreneurship-programs.
83  "Entrepreneurship Funds and Resources for People under 30," Government of Ontario, accessed November 11, 2014, https://www.ontario.ca/jobs-and-employment/entrepreneurship-funds-and-resources-people-under-30.
84  Creso Sá and Hana Lee, "Science, Business, and Innovation: Understanding Networks in Technology-Based Incubators," *R&D Management* 42, no. 3 (2012): 243–253.

85  Ministry of Training, Colleges and Universities, *Ontario's Differentiation Policy Framework for Postsecondary Education* (Toronto: Queen's Printer for Ontario, 2013).

86  "Advanced Manufacturing," *Illinois Department of Commerce and Economic Opportunity*, accessed November 11, 2014, http://www.illinois.gov/dceo/whyillinois/KeyIndustries/AdvancedManufacturing/Pages/default.aspx.

87  "Illinois Innovation Ecosystem," *Illinois Innovation Network,* accessed November 23, 2014, http://www.illinoisinnovation.com/illinois-innovation-ecosystem.

88  "Governor Quinn Announces Creation of Illinois Innovation Council," *Illinois Government News Network*, February 16, 2011, accessed November 15, 2014, http://www3.illinois.gov/PressReleases/ShowPressRelease.cfm?SubjectID=2&RecNum=9226.

89  "About the Network," *Illinois Innovation Network*, accessed November 15, 2014, http://www.illinoisinnovation.com/about-the-network.

90  "ChicagoNEXT," *World Business Chicago*, accessed on November 11, 2014, https://www.worldbusinesschicago.com/chicagonext; "Mayor Emanuel Launches ChicagoNEXT To Amplify City's Tech and Science Business Climate," *City of Chicago, Mayor's Press Office*, October, 16, 2012, accessed October 20, 2014, http://www.cityofchicago.org/city/en/depts/mayor/press_room/press_releases/2012/october_2012/mayor_emanuel_launcheschicagonexttoamplifycitystechandsciencebus.html.

91  "Governor Quinn Announces MATTER, A New Healthcare Technology Startup Hub," *Illinois Innovation Network*, accessed February 6, 2014, http://www3.illinois.gov/pressreleases/ShowPressRelease.cfm?SubjectID=2&RecNum=11929.

92  John Pletz, "Illinois, U of I Launching Life-Sciences Startup Incubator in Chicago," *Crain's Chicago Business,* April 22, 2013, accessed November 28, 2014, http://www.chicagobusiness.com/article/20130422/BLOGS11/130429980/illinois-u-of-i-launching-life-sciences-startup-incubator-in-chicago.

93  Jim Kendall, "New Program Focuses on Higher Tech Businesses," Kendall Communications Inc., accessed November 11, 2014, http://kendallcom.com/your-tax-dollars-at-work/.

94  Brian Richard, Joey Lata, Jennifer Groce, Norman Walzer, Brian Harger, and Andy Blanke, *Sustainable Funding for Early State Small Businesses in the State of Ingenuity: An Analysis of Business Readiness for Capitalization* (A Report to the United States Economic Development Agency), March 2014, accessed December 4, 2014, http://cgs.niu.edu/Reports/Access_to_Capital_Final.pdf; "State of Ingenuity," *SourceLink*, accessed November 8, 2014, http://www.ussourcelink.com/docs/default-source/our-affiliates-pdfs/soisourcelink.pdf?sfvrsn=2.

95 Kevin Kiley, "The New York Tax Advantage," *Inside HigherEd*, August 14, 2013, accessed October 14, 2014, http://www.insidehighered.com/news/2013/08/14/new-yorks-tax-free-plan-puts-suny-center-economic-development.

96 Charles Brown, James Hamilton, and James Medoff, *Employers Large and Small* (Cambridge, MA: Harvard University Press, 1990).

97 Scott Shane, *Illusions of Entrepreneurship* (New Haven, CT: Yale University Press, 2008).

98 Simon C. Parker, *The Economics of Entrepreneurship* (Cambridge: Cambridge University Press, 2009), 226, 407–409.

99 Parker, *The Economics of Entrepreneurship*.

100 Susan Clark Muntean, "Embracing Entrepreneurship," *Indiana Business Review*, Spring 2011, accessed October 23, 2014, http://www.ibrc.indiana.edu/ibr/2011/spring/article1.html.

101 According to Economist Peter Armstrong, "the figure of the entrepreneurs serves as a *deus ex machine*" within policy making and current political ideology; "[a]s a policy for the commercial exploitation of science...the nurture of entrepreneurship is not so much a solution as the expression of a wish [that] one would appear" [Peter Armstrong, "Science, Enterprise and Profit: Ideology in the Knowledge-Driven Economy," *Economy and Society* 30, no. 4 (2001): 526].

# 4
# Entrepreneurship Learning on Campus

**Abstract:** *This chapter investigates the efforts being undertaken in higher education to teach entrepreneurship and impart entrepreneurial attitudes and values to students. The chapter charts the development of entrepreneurship education and examines its diffusion from business schools across college and university campuses. Accompanying the growing diversity and number of entrepreneurship courses and degree programs are a range of extracurricular programming, such as innovative incubation programs, start-up workshops, and new venture seed funds. The development of entrepreneurship education at four universities is examined in depth and reveals how the curricular and extracurricular opportunities for students to learn entrepreneurship are often responses to internal and external influences. Overall, the chapter identifies the diversification of models employed inside and outside the classroom to impart entrepreneurial mindsets and skills to students.*

Sá, Creso M. and Andrew J. Kretz. *The Entrepreneurship Movement and the University.* New York: Palgrave Macmillan, 2015. DOI: 10.1057/9781137401014.0007.

Thirty years ago, entrepreneurship education proponent Robert Ronstadt argued sanguinely, "Can entrepreneurship be taught? Can it be learned? The debate continues unabated in the press, at academic conferences, and even meetings of successful practitioners. The continued dialogue is worthwhile but the decision has already been made. Entrepreneurship will be taught and students have chosen in large numbers to learn about starting new ventures and other topics associated increasingly with the emerging field of [e]ntrepreneurial [s]tudies."[1] Although the debate as to whether or not entrepreneurship can be taught is ongoing to this day, the notion that colleges and universities should provide entrepreneurial learning opportunities has become well established on campuses across Canada and the United States.

The first entrepreneurship course was introduced at Harvard University in 1947. It was not until the early 1970s, however, that entrepreneurship education began to gain a firm foothold in higher education,[2] and during the 1980s, the number of entrepreneurship courses doubled.[3] During this period of growth, many scholars were critical of entrepreneurship education, with many questioning whether entrepreneurship could even be taught.[4] Despite these challenges to the growth of entrepreneurship education, the field continued to expand. Most recent estimates—already several years dated—place the number of entrepreneurship courses offered in US colleges and universities at over 1,600.[5] Some of these courses are offered at community colleges, which first established entrepreneurship courses in the late 1970s and experienced rapid growth thereafter.[6] By 2004, 62 percent of American community colleges were offering one or more courses in small business or entrepreneurship.[7] In Canada, a similar trend has occurred, where the number of entrepreneurship courses offered at universities grew from 72 in 1979 to 351 by the middle of the 2000s.[8] Most universities in Canada now offer at least one course in entrepreneurship, and large research institutions boast multiple offerings.[9]

Accompanying the rise in course offerings, institutions of higher education in both the United States and Canada have introduced entrepreneurship degrees, certificates, and specialization programs. The first entrepreneurship programs were launched at the University of Southern California: the Master of Business Administration (MBA) concentration in entrepreneurship in 1971, followed by the first undergraduate concentration a year later.[10] By the mid-1980s, there were ten programs offering an entrepreneurship specialization in the

United States and Canada: at the University of Southern California, the Wharton School at the University of Pennsylvania, Babson College, Baylor University, Northeastern University, Wichita State University, the University of California, Los Angeles, and Harvard University in the United States; and at York University and the University of Calgary in Canada.[11]

Although the development of entrepreneurship education programs was not initially embraced, they are now common in higher education. Scholars and entrepreneurs alike argue that students require more than coursework to succeed as entrepreneurs. Entrepreneurship, after all, is an applied discipline, and its unpredictable nature requires that students apply and reflect on course learning and actual practice.[12] Entrepreneurial practice addresses what numerous entrepreneurship educators have emphasized—that students should take ownership of their learning, undertake business planning, solve problems in real-world situations, and develop relations with mentors and other practitioners.[13]

Accordingly, universities have sought to provide these practical experiences. A growing number of opportunities for students interested in entrepreneurship, or would-be entrepreneurs, populate American and Canadian campuses. Entrepreneurship conferences, workshops, and boot camps seek to help students develop their ideas within a lower-stakes environment, and in the company of like-minded peers. Several universities have also established university venture funds, some fully or partly funded with university resources, from which to provide capital to student ventures. Some universities have even created an Entrepreneur-in-Residence position to provide consulting, networking, mentoring, and coaching to student entrepreneurs. In addition, several universities house residence halls or living-learning communities centered on entrepreneurship in attempts to foster the development of student entrepreneur communities. These diverse initiatives demonstrate the increasing importance of entrepreneurialism in higher education.

Growing support and interest in entrepreneurship education has prompted universities and colleges to integrate entrepreneurial learning throughout campuses and beyond the conventional confines of the business school. Through this process, entrepreneurship is being redefined as a multidisciplinary approach that serves the goals of multiple fields.

## Entrepreneurship as a field of study

Although entrepreneurship courses and programs are typically found within business schools, entrepreneurship education is largely its own field of study—fundamental differences exist between the business principles applied to new ventures and those applied to large corporations.[14] Rather than emphasize principles of commerce and business management, entrepreneurship education has as its core opportunity recognition and exploitation, and business and market entry.[15] Differences also exist between entrepreneurship and small business management, although the two terms are often used interchangeably. According to entrepreneurship scholar Donald Kuratko, entrepreneurs and small-business owners have different perspectives on the development of their companies. Namely, whereas "small-business owners can be viewed as *managers* of small businesses" and generally expect stable sales, profits, and growth, entrepreneurs seek rapid growth and immediate profits through innovative strategies and practices.[16]

Apart from these general distinctions, conceptions of entrepreneurship vary,[17] and there has been little agreement in the field about the competencies or skills that are most valuable for aspiring entrepreneurs to learn.[18] Jerome Katz, an entrepreneurship professor at the University of St Louis, argues that there has been a general convergence around topics included in entrepreneurship courses.[19] Basically, courses reflect the challenges entrepreneurs face, rather than conventional business disciplines, such as marketing or finance, and programs are structured around the milestones in the creation and growth of start-ups.[20] This involves topics such as identifying a potential opportunity, conducting market feasibility analysis, planning the new venture, and securing financing. Proponents of entrepreneurship programs contend that students should be learning *for* entrepreneurship rather than *about* it. The first implies learning relevant skills and techniques on how to be an entrepreneur. In courses following this approach, the curriculum is designed around business planning, the entrepreneurial process (the issues, requirements, and tools for different stages in venture creation), and the venture life cycle.[21] Common university course titles are Introduction to Entrepreneurship, Small Business Management, New Venture Creation, and Business Plan Development.[22] More recent offerings includes Entrepreneurial Thinking and Behavior; Entrepreneurial Marketing; Social Entrepreneurship; Corporate Entrepreneurship; Entrepreneurship and Innovation,

Entrepreneurship and New Technologies; New Product Development; and Innovation Management.[23]

Entrepreneurship is thus not directed toward a specific career or pathway, but oriented toward different forms of problem-solving. As part of this orientation, entrepreneurship education normally seeks to blend theory and practice. Guest speakers and case studies are common in entrepreneurship courses, and course assignments are often organized around group projects.[24] The hallmark of most entrepreneurship education courses is the writing of a business plan, which often serves as the major assignment in a course or a capstone project in a program.[25] Business plans critically analyze the proposed business concept and all other relevant aspects connected with the creation and development of the proposed venture—its product or service, its industry, its market, its manner of operating, and its financial outcomes.[26]

Business plans are so popular that many universities and colleges now host or participate in business plan competitions.[27] Business plan competitions on individual campuses began in the early 1980s, and were followed by national competitions in the second half of the decade.[28] During the 1990s participation in business plan competitions increased.[29] A 2006 survey of 2,100 universities found that over 300 institutions offered business plan competitions.[30] It is not uncommon for universities to host more than one competition. At the University of Ottawa, for instance, the Faculty of Engineering hosts two competitions, dubbed "Entrepreneurship Concepts" and "Launching Entrepreneurs." The first is intended for students with burgeoning ideas. By enrolling in the faculty's technology entrepreneurship course in the fall, participating students develop an idea to be presented in the competition in the spring.[31] Several university competitions have adopted this approach, where applicants have the opportunity to attend courses or workshops where they are guided in developing and refining their business concepts, before they make a final presentation. Whereas the Entrepreneurship Concepts Competition is intended to foster an entrepreneurial culture among students, the Launching Entrepreneurs competition aims to support students with companies that already have a customer base.[32] Other institutions offer multiple competitions tailored to certain specialties. For example, at the University of Southern California, business plan competitions emphasize "new media" companies (YPrize New Media Competition), digital media and technology (Silicon Beach), and consumer products and lifestyle enterprises (Student Innovator Showcase).[33]

Entrepreneurship courses and programs are often supported by entrepreneurship centers. Most centers were established after the mid-1990s.[34] The number of centers in American universities and colleges has grown from around 100 in the early 2000s to 249 in 2012.[35] In Canada, there are approximately 30 centers, most of which are affiliated with business schools.[36] Many entrepreneurship centers have established advisory boards comprised of advocates for entrepreneurship representing industry, business, finance, and the not-for-profit sector to provide ongoing guidance and support. Although the mission of centers was originally to provide business extension services targeting small businesses, they moved to support education and training programs as part of their efforts to support entrepreneurial activity. This includes extracurricular activities such as involving students in research; providing experiential learning opportunities; providing consulting, mentoring, and networking for students on venture launch and business plan preparation; providing workshops or seminars for students on new venture creation and planning; sponsoring student clubs; and managing venture capital funds.[37]

More recently, universities have moved to further institutionalize entrepreneurship in the academic structure through dedicated departments and schools. In some universities, existing departments have been reorganized to include an emphasis on entrepreneurship, while at other institutions new units have been created. The first school of entrepreneurship in the United States was established at the Oklahoma State University in 2012. The school's offerings in the field include minors for nonbusiness students and for business majors, a major, an MBA concentration, and a doctoral program. The school houses the Riata Center for Entrepreneurship that runs a range of outreach programs, including entrepreneurship bootcamps, internships, and business plan competitions.[38] The University of North Dakota was the second public university to establish a School of Entrepreneurship in 2014, which joined similar units at three private universities: University of St Thomas, Drexel University, and Bradley University.[39]

Student clubs focused on the topic have also increased across campuses.[40] Examples of national student organizations include Enactus, Collegiate Entrepreneurs' Organization, Enterprize Canada, Collegiate DECA (formerly Delta Epsilon Chi), and the entrepreneurship honors society Sigma Nu Tau, that support local chapters and host national and regional conferences and expositions, competitions, and awards. Typical activities that these clubs undertake include hosting guest lecturers, and panel discussions as well as sponsoring and running workshops, competitions, and networking events.[41]

## University-wide entrepreneurship education

The expansion of entrepreneurial studies has sparked experimentation among colleges and universities in the types of structures, pedagogical models, and extracurricular supports they make available to students. Apart from entrepreneurship centers and academic units focused on the field, several institutions have sought to promote entrepreneurial learning across the campus through cross-departmental approaches. This experimentation is partly supported by a number of organizations that support field-building activities in the area of entrepreneurship. Some university initiatives seek to disseminate best practices, such as the Experiential Learning Program at University of Florida, the Symposium for Entrepreneurship Educators at Babson College, and the Roundtable for Entrepreneurship Educators at Stanford University.[42] In the United States, the United States Association for Small Business and Entrepreneurship's (USASBE) annual conference provides a platform for the dissemination of new insights into entrepreneurship education pedagogy.[43] The USASBE also runs the National Model Program Awards to recognize outstanding programs in higher education.[44] The Global Consortium of Entrepreneurship Centers, whose global character is overshadowed by the overwhelming membership of US universities, has the NASDAQ Center of Excellence awards for similar ends.[45] The Kern Entrepreneurship Education Network, run by the Kern Family Foundation, is a collaboration of 20 private universities across the United States that is working to instill an entrepreneurial mindset in undergraduate engineering and technology students.[46]

Entrepreneurship education is reflected in various institutional models. One is a focused model, in which entrepreneurship education is administered within one or more departments or schools exclusively for students enrolled in those programs. Another falls under university-wide programs that are either a centrally run or managed by multiple academic units.[47] For example, an entrepreneurship center may serve as a base for programs and courses for students across the campus. This form is probably the most common among university-wide entrepreneurship efforts today.

The trend toward university-wide entrepreneurship education is strong and gaining momentum among universities in the United States and Canada. In both countries, many universities are incorporating the ethos of entrepreneurship into institutional missions.[48] Engineering schools, and some science and technology programs, were the first to incorporate entrepreneurship into coursework. The US National Academy of Sciences and the American Society for Engineering Education each promote the teaching of entrepreneurial competencies to science and engineering students. Engineers, after all, are often employed by large firms to work in research and development, where entrepreneurship is central to uncovering and developing the technological innovations that lead to firm growth and renewal.[49] A little over half of engineering schools at American Society for Engineering Education member institutions (341) offer some type of undergraduate entrepreneurship program. However, students from across the disciplinary spectrum can now more easily complete a minor in entrepreneurship.[50] A number of universities and colleges have introduced entrepreneurship courses in academic departments such as psychology, geography, earth, environmental science, fine and performing arts, and music.

Many campus-wide entrepreneurship initiatives are bolstered with external support, particularly in the United States. The number of endowed faculty positions outside of business schools has grown dramatically in the United States, and are now found in schools of engineering, agriculture, arts and sciences, and other more specialized professional schools.[51] Foundations have supported the curricular integration of entrepreneurship into general undergraduate education, quite prominently in the case of the Kauffman Foundation. The Coleman Foundation's Faculty Entrepreneurship Fellows Program has sponsored faculty who teach in disciplines outside the school of business.[52] Further promoting entrepreneurship on campuses is VentureWell.[53] Through its University Innovation Fellows program, funded by the National Science Foundation and run in partnership with Stanford University, VentureWell trains and supports students in expanding innovation and entrepreneurship opportunities on their campuses. Advocating for the support of social entrepreneurs on campus is Ashoka, a nonprofit organization focused on promoting social entrepreneurship. Through its Ashoka U initiative, the organization works with university officials and administrators to develop programs that foster campus-wide cultures of social innovation.[54]

These developments do not suggest that the increasing prominence of entrepreneurship on campuses occurs without being contested. That is, the integration of entrepreneurship into nonbusiness programs has encountered resistance from faculty members and deans. When asked about their views on incorporating entrepreneurship into university curricula, many faculty members did not believe that the subject was compatible with the mission and intellectual traditions of their particular school or department, and they believed that it would become a distraction from education and professional training objectives.[55] Nevertheless, advocates of entrepreneurship have in many cases quelled resistance by highlighting how entrepreneurial skills and thinking support competencies necessary for life-long learning and critical thinking,[56] as well as civic engagement, leadership, and social change.[57] These arguments in favor of entrepreneur education have contributed to entrepreneurship emphases in several fields.

## Arts entrepreneurship

Since the late 1990s there has been a concerted effort in the United States to link arts and entrepreneurship disciplines.[58] The Association of Arts Administration Educators (AAAE) and USASBE, for example, have embraced arts entrepreneurship as a segment of larger disciplines. Rather than training professionals to work in existing arts organizations, arts entrepreneurship focuses on teaching artists how to apply entrepreneurial skills and techniques to advance their careers. This translates into teaching artists about recognizing opportunities, communicating with audiences, securing funding, and marketing their projects.[59] According to members of the USASBE Arts Entrepreneurship Special Interest Group, there are an estimated 450 arts entrepreneurship courses.[60] Some institutions may elect, as has UW-Madison, to develop an arts entrepreneurship focus within a business school. Others may support entrepreneurship curriculum and programming from within an arts college or institute, as was done at Arizona State University. Some universities are now offering arts entrepreneurship minors, typically through Arts Administration programs. At the North Carolina State University, however, students from all majors who are interested in exploring entrepreneurial opportunities in the arts and arts-related fields may complete a minor in arts entrepreneurship.[61]

## Liberal arts

Dozens of scholars have highlighted the parallels between an education for the development of entrepreneurial mindsets and a liberal arts education.[62] These scholars argue that a liberal arts education offers the opportunity for a holistic educational experience that is well suited to the needs of the potential entrepreneur, primarily because the would-be entrepreneur needs to encounter a wide variety of perspectives, paradigms of inquiry, and ethical norms and develop critical thinking and communication skills.[63] Sociologist Mary Godwyn has noted the commonalities between the goals of the liberal arts and of entrepreneurship. She argues that "entrepreneurship is a tangible, practical manifestation of a liberal arts sensibility."[64] Likewise, others claim that entrepreneurship education not only serves a similar purpose as the liberal arts—it teaches students to approach problems in novel ways, allows them to develop a comfort with ambiguity—but also encourages students to apply their learning in practical contexts. Moreover, entrepreneurship education teaches a student how to think rather than what to think.[65] Writing as dean of the School of Humanities and Social Sciences at the College of Charleston, Samuel M. Hines Jr opined, "[t]he ideal liberal arts education models a process of continuous adaptation and innovation that is manifest in one's personal and professional life", and that is commensurate with the study and practice of entrepreneurship.[66] Similarly, Henry G. Rennie, Professor of Economics at Heidelberg College, sees entrepreneurship as a creative act well suited for liberal arts colleges and "fundamental to the liberal arts vision of integrating learning and life."[67]

## Social entrepreneurship

The synergy between community-based service learning and entrepreneurship has empowered social entrepreneurship.[68] Social entrepreneurs aim to employ economic and market-driven solutions for solving social problems.[69] They are often defined as change agents that emphasize the creation of social rather than economic value.[70] In addition, social entrepreneurship is consistent with the broader movement toward corporate social and environmental responsibility.[71] Social entrepreneurship became a topic of study in the early 1990s,[72] and was characterized by activity and courses primarily at graduate schools of business, with Harvard University, Stanford University, Columbia University, and other well-respected university business programs as among the early leaders.[73] There was a significant increase in attention to social entrepreneurship in the 2000s, as evidenced by the growth in university courses and programs.[74] By 2005 nearly 32 percent of the 47 ranked undergraduate business programs of the US News and World Report annual rankings offered either a formal program of study or individual courses in social entrepreneurship.[75] Since 2005, social entrepreneurship has expanded from business schools to other schools on university and college campuses, with an array of disciplines taking ownership of social entrepreneurship and social innovation.[76] There are now also social entrepreneurship programs, majors, minors, and certificates at universities throughout the United States and Canada.[77] The emergence of social entrepreneurship is also recognized through competitions, such as the Global Social Venture Competition at the University of California, Berkeley, during which social entrepreneurs present venture ideas for a chance to win start-up money and prizes. Other cocurricular programs mirror those formed to support business venture entrepreneurs, as discussed below.

## Experiential learning

As noted earlier, entrepreneurship experts advocate that programs educate "for" entrepreneurship rather than "about" it.[78] These advocates of entrepreneurship education have long argued that the best methods suited for educating future entrepreneurs are action-oriented simulations built around challenging, realistic, and hands-on experiences.[79] Instead of teaching students how to write business plans, which some criticize as too hypothetical a practice,[80] new approaches to entrepreneurship education have focused on providing real experiences that are based on actual interactions in the marketplace.

One popular approach to supporting students in the creation of their own ventures is the "Lean Startup." According to Steve Blank, a serial-entrepreneur and lecturer at the University of California Berkeley Haas School of Business who has popularized the method, the Learn Startup methodology "favors experimentation over elaborate planning, customer feedback over intuition, and iterative design over traditional 'big design up front' development."[81] Instead of business plans, students summarize the assumptions they hold for their venture in a framework called the business model canvas—a one-page diagram that shows how their company creates value for itself and its customers.[82] Students then show the company's "minimum viable product" (a version of a new product containing only critical features) to potential users, producers, and partners for feedback. Using the input they receive, students reflect on the assumptions of their business model and make any necessary changes, or "pivots."[83] By testing their assumptions on a weekly basis, students discover whether their desired customers would actually buy or use their products, and they learn firsthand about the start-up process.

Entrepreneurship program administrators have been enthusiastic adopters of the Lean Startup method and its underlying concepts. Advocates of this model for teaching entrepreneurship are introducing competitions based on students' business models, rather than business plans.[84] These events are known as "pitch competitions," and have students "pitching" their incipient businesses within a few minutes to successful entrepreneurs, angel investors, and venture capitalists. These events are sometimes referred to as "elevator pitch" competitions because they "capture the ability of an entrepreneur to have his or her business concept defined so precisely that they could walk into an elevator, find that they are standing next to a potential investor, and convey the essence of their business by the time the elevator gets to the 20th floor."[85] Other than showcasing students' ideas and encouraging an entrepreneurial culture on campus, these competitions aim to provide training, mentoring, and networking opportunities to student participants. In addition to bringing together students with the entrepreneur community, pitch competitions, such as the Lavin VentureStart Competition hosted by San Diego State University's Lavin Entrepreneurship center, has participants attend start-up workshops before submitting their final business model to the competition.[86]

This ethos of combining classroom learning with real-life entrepreneurial practice corresponds to university initiatives aimed at extending entrepreneurial thinking and practice to contexts outside of the classroom. Seeking to expose students to entrepreneurial mindsets and orientations within like-minded communities, universities have created special on-campus living arrangements for those interested in the field. They have done so drawing on the established practice of designating "living learning communities" around entrepreneurship. Living learning communities are residence halls where undergraduate students live together and participate in structured programming throughout the year, designed around particular themes or interests. In addition to a shared residence hall, students typically have access to on-site classes, workshops, workspaces, and other entrepreneurship-related amenities and activities, causing some to dub these programs "dormcubators."[87] The primary goals of entrepreneurship living-learning communities are to contribute to an entrepreneurial spirit on campus by creating a sense of community and cooperation, and nurture the aspiring entrepreneurs earlier in their academic careers. Residential learning communities are known to improve participating students' levels of involvement, interaction, and integration, as well as their gains in learning and intellectual development.[88] Such communities also make entrepreneurship and the entrepreneurship opportunities on campus, more visible to students from different disciplines. Communities are generally open to students from all faculties and programs.

The first entrepreneurship living-learning program was offered in 2000 at University of Maryland, College Park. Dozens of universities and colleges now support these communities.[89] Many programs are the result of collaboration between university housing and entrepreneurship programs or centers, and schools of business or engineering. For example, the Innovation residence learning community at the Wilfred Laurier University partners with the university's Schlegel Centre for Entrepreneurship, the Student Leadership Centre, and the Career Centre in hosting workshops for students. Such partnerships on campus are not just functional but also strategic. For instance, at the University of Illinois, Urbana-Champaign, the Technology Entrepreneur Center partnered with University Housing and created the Innovation living-learning community as a way to reach freshman and sophomore students and exposing them to entrepreneurial thinking. Taking the concept of the living-learning community further, the University of Florida has recently begun constructing a residence building for a new entrepreneurial-based academic residential community that will include spaces for faculty research, entrepreneurs, and incubators at its location at the university's Innovation Square.[90]

Additionally, universities are promoting practical entrepreneurial learning through study abroad opportunities. Such opportunities typically allow undergraduate students to spend a semester abroad to learn relevant subject matter while benefiting from immersion in a different culture. Some universities host summer abroad experiences that combine coursework with participation in intensive start-up workshops. The University of California, Berkeley, for instance, offers a summer abroad experience for its students that combines coursework with participation in the European Innovation Academy—an annual, 15-day technology start-up boot-camp.[91] Others may have students meet with entrepreneurs abroad to learn about opportunities and challenges of developing ventures in different national and regional contexts. Students from Purdue University, for example, learn about entrepreneurship, innovation, and product development during a two-week trip to China. Baylor University offers short-term study abroad, opportunities to learn about entrepreneurial practice in Europe, Costa Rica, and Rwanda.[92] Reflecting the trend discussed above, some universities combine service learning and social entrepreneurship projects to build sustainable ventures or consulting activities in developing regions. At the University of Connecticut, students may travel to Guatemala to learn about the country's language and culture and partner with nongovernmental organizations in supporting local entrepreneurs. During this eight-week program, up to 20 students combine coursework with an internship with field professionals and social entrepreneurs in Guatemala to help develop small businesses.[93]

## Helping student become entrepreneurs

Together with the experiential learning opportunities discussed earlier, universities are keen to help their students become entrepreneurs. Through structured extracurricular programs, they seek to provide students with the venues for them to move from aspiration to actual engagement in launching a venture. A growing ecosystem of related programming is available to university students, including start-up weekends, meetups, and hackdays or hackathons.

Start-up summits and start-up weekends provide a hybrid between a conference and a start-up competition, in which entrepreneurs convene for a few days to network, form teams, and launch a venture. For these kinds of events, students usually meet for the first time on a Friday afternoon to begin developing an idea, and work throughout the weekend to transform it into a product or prototype. At the end of the event, teams present the product of their efforts to a panel of judges, giving them an opportunity to win cash and other prizes. Nonprofit organizations such as Startup Weekend help to facilitate the organization of many of these events although universities may play host as well.[94] Students at Queen's

University in Kingston, Ontario, spearheaded the school's first Startup Summit, at which students from universities across Ontario and Quebec came together in Kingston to launch a start-up over the span of a weekend.[95] In the United States, Princeton University students have hosted an East Coast Start-Up Summit to connect student entrepreneurs from the regions' universities during a weekend of workshops, seminars, and networking events.[96]

Many aspiring entrepreneurs are interested in a quick competition cycle where they can form teams, identify a problem, and create a solution—all in a few hours or days. Hackathons are events at which student developers, designers, and entrepreneurs form teams to produce mobile apps and web programs to address real-world challenges. They convene around broad themes released prior to the competition, develop product mock-ups, and pitch their team's creation by the end of the weekend. At the end of the hackathon, there is usually a series of demonstrations in which each group presents their results. There is sometimes a contest element as well, in which a panel of judges select the winning teams, and prizes are given.[97] Many hackathons are sponsored collaboratively by universities and external organizations. The University of Calgary, for instance, partners with the local entrepreneurship community to host Hackhealth, focused on health care innovations, where health professionals team with developers and designers. Student groups are also responsible for the proliferation of hackathons. HackSC is one such student group, consisting of students at the University of Southern California. At neighboring UCLA, students hosted "LA Hacks," where a reported 1,500 university students from UCLA and beyond worked in teams over the weekend to create and present "apps" for prizes and awards.[98]

For students creating a venture, some universities and colleges have established mentoring programs. Most mentors are volunteers and are typically entrepreneurs who in many cases are also alumni. These mentors guide students through the process of starting a business while helping to identify market opportunities and areas for improvement. Moreover, they act as role models and encourage risk-taking, providing encouragement during inevitable setbacks and changes that accompany venture creation.[99] In addition to serving as mentors, these community entrepreneurs also provide guest lectures, judge competitions, host student interns, evaluate programs, and serve as board members on student start-ups or on advisory boards of entrepreneurship programs.[100]

Outside organizations also provide this kind of support and are welcomed on campuses. In Canada, *The Next 36* is a program that selects 36 undergraduates from a variety of academic disciplines to build businesses oriented toward mobile phones or tablet devices. For eight months they are provided mentorship from business leaders, access to funding from venture capitalists, and supportive resources and academic instruction at the "Entrepreneurship Institute" in Toronto. In the United States, VentureWell coordinates the E-Team Program, in which multidisciplinary groups of students, faculty, and industry mentors are funded to bring a technology-based invention to market. VentureWell also hosts an annual conference, competitions for biomedical and bioengineering students, and multiple programs and grants to support faculty in the creation of new entrepreneurship courses and programs.[101] The Collegiate Entrepreneurs' Organization, a student entrepreneur network with chapters at 245 colleges and universities, provides student entrepreneurs with opportunities, events, chapter activities, and conferences to help start businesses.[102] Many other organizations, such as FounderDating and Startup Canada provide networking opportunities where students can meet other entrepreneurs, developers, designers, product managers, and investors. These organizations are part of an increasingly diverse ecosystem supporting entrepreneurialism in higher education.

## Nurturing student start-ups

Student entrepreneurs increasingly find an array of initiatives on campuses where they can develop their start-ups. The most accessible way of supporting students with entrepreneurial ambitions is by creating spaces for students to experiment with new ideas and connect with business mentors, investors, and other support. These spaces are commonly known as hatcheries or sandboxes, and support students informally and at their own pace. These spaces generally include shared facilities, such as offices and conference rooms. A faculty member or an administrator oversees the space, coordinating events and connecting students. By making such a space open to students with even just a vague idea for a venture, these spaces support the development of an entrepreneurship ecosystem and community on campus.[103]

Campus-based incubators are another supportive environment for developing student entrepreneurs and their start-ups. Unlike hatcheries, however, incubators seek to help new start-ups survive and grow, welcoming students with more developed business ideas with a range of supports and services.[104] Incubators frequently rent subsidized office space for start-ups, where entrepreneurs have access to shared facilities and resources. They are thus relatively more complex (although still "lean") operations than hatcheries, entailing not just a manager and staff, but also an advisory board, industry contacts, and professional services providers such as lawyers, venture capitalists, and angel investors. Participating students are typically in the earlier-stages of venture development, and are normally accepted into the incubator after an application process in which they must present a business plan and a prototype of their product.

While incubators may host start-ups for the first few years in the ventures' life, accelerators are generally short-term, intensive programs aimed at helping a cohort of entrepreneurs make critical progress in launching and growing their businesses. Usually lasting a few months, accelerators provide entrepreneurs with a plethora of networking, educational, and mentoring opportunities. These may include advisers who might be successful entrepreneurs, corporate executives, program graduates, as well as financiers such as angel investors and venture capitalists. Accelerators are less focused on providing the typical infrastructure of incubators, such as office space and shared facilities, and more invested into the capitalization or revenue growth of fledgling companies. A "demo day" is the usual culmination of accelerator programs, where participating entrepreneurs present their businesses to investors.[105]

At some institutions, entrepreneurship courses, hatcheries, incubators, and accelerators may be viewed as "a funnel, a ladder, or a pipeline," through which students may progress.[106] The Kauffman Foundation likens this process to musical education, "which begins with music appreciation classes for practically everyone and extends through conservatory training for the especially talented few."[107] For example, students might take an idea formed during a course to an on-campus hatchery for development before moving on to an incubator, and maybe even to an accelerator after that. Obviously, not all programs follow the distinctions made above, and the lines between forms of start-up support can be blurred to share features of each of the models. Moreover, universities and colleges may only have one or two of the above spaces, which might not be formally connected to one another.

Most campus-based incubators and accelerators specialize in the creation of digital technology companies. However, as the entrepreneurship movement develops, campus-based incubators have begun to diversify. At the University of Waterloo, students may take their business ideas to Velocity Garage, a conventional incubator space, or else to Velocity Science, for those with ventures focused on biology, chemistry, physics, and earth and environmental sciences. For students who need to build hardware for their start-ups, the Velocity Foundry provides the equipment and mentorship necessary to develop, test, and implement their start-up ideas.[108] Facilities where students can build prototypes are often called "makerspaces," and they have emerged at universities and colleges across the United States and Canada. Although not always directly connected to entrepreneurship education programs, campus makerspaces provide students access to a prototyping facility that includes 3D printers, a machine shop and other engineering equipment to enable the development of both digital and physical products.

A smaller number of universities have established programs that encourage arts venture incubation. Arts incubators are similar to regular incubators, except they may not be founded with similar economic development expectations. Instead, "individual self-efficacy and entrepreneurial thinking about the arts and creative industries are primary goals."[109] The Pave Arts Venture Incubator housed with Arizona State's School of Film, Dance, and Theatre is one of eight university arts incubator programs or university extension programs in the United States,[110] and each year it provides seed funding for up to six teams that receive assistance with the development of a project proposal. Similar programs exist in Canada. At OCAD University, Canada's largest and oldest educational institution for art and design, Imagination Catalyst is the university's entrepreneurship and commercialization hub. It offers students a chance to participate in the Take-It-to-Market incubator; if accepted, students or recent graduates commit to working on their venture full-time for up to one year. Participants are provided a full-range of support services and are given access to shared meeting spaces, event/presentation venues, and fabrication/prototyping facilities.[111]

To help students launch their ventures, entrepreneurship programs may connect students with local angel investors and venture capitalists. Many universities and colleges are also directly providing students with start-up capital in several formats. One is the prize money awarded to winners of business plan and pitch competitions; another is start-up funding for students accepted into accelerator programs; and yet another is funding from grants programs setup with financial gifts from donors.[112] At the University of Waterloo, the Velocity Fund is one such grant program for start-ups and aspiring student entrepreneurs. Furthermore, several universities have established venture capital funds to support the commercialization of university research. The University of Illinois at Chicago launched the Chancellor's Innovation Fund to help move technologies developed by faculty, students or staff from research to commercial use.[113] Drexel University created "Drexel Ventures," a seed funding, incubation and technology transfer enterprise that supports proof-of-concept projects that move faculty and student inventions closer to market, and provides seed capital for start-ups to commercialize them. The NYU Innovation Venture Fund is a seed-stage venture capital that invests in start-ups founded by current NYU students, faculty, and researchers. Even universities known for their entrepreneurial bent have sought to provide this kind of support to aspiring student entrepreneurs. Stanford University plans to invest in students' companies housed in StartX, a nonprofit start-up accelerator for Stanford-affiliated entrepreneurs.[114] In 2014, the University of California announced plans for a new venture-capital fund to finance start-ups created by faculty and students on its campuses.[115]

In another approach to financing start-ups, several universities are turning to crowdfunding platforms. Crowdfunding refers to efforts by entrepreneurial individuals and groups—cultural, social, and for-profit—to fund their ventures by drawing on relatively small contributions from a large number of individuals without standard financial intermediaries.[116] Since the 2012 Jumpstart Our Business Startups (JOBS) Act was passed in the United States, crowdfunding has become an additional means of soliciting investment capital and providing equity to start-ups.[117] The JOBS Act encourages funding of small businesses by easing securities regulations for individual investors and business start-ups, and allows start-ups to sell securities through online, open platforms or funding portals. Crowdfunding campaigns normally include a webpage containing a description of the product idea or business, funding goals, a demonstration video, and a social media campaign to engage and attract supporters.[118] Georgia Tech Research Institute (GTRI) researcher Allison Mercer founded Georgia Tech Starter, a university-based crowdfunding platform for science and engineering projects.[119] Launcht, a crowdfunding platform catering to universities and colleges, has partnered with the

University of Vermont to create UVMStart to fund student start-ups. Launcht also set up a "crowdvoting" platform for Southern Illinois University's business idea competition.[120] Crowdfunding goes beyond offering a means to fund early stage ideas. Online platforms provide a vehicle from which students connect with potential investors and users. During the process of seeking funding, student entrepreneurs may test and refine their ideas, practice their pitches, and learn how to engage with potential future users.[121]

Georgetown University has taken a unique approach to funding student entrepreneurs. Starting in 2015, graduating students can compete for stipends up to the amount of their student loan debt to assist them in launching an entrepreneurial venture. The goal of the Startup Stipend program is to encourage students to pursue entrepreneurship by removing the need of finding immediate employment after graduation, as the financial obligation of student loan debt may dissuade would-be entrepreneurs from taking the risk of venture creation. Recipients of the stipend can use the money to support costs associated with their start-up or pay off their school loans.[122]

Despite their growing presence on university campuses, evidence of the effect of university venture capital funding is inconclusive. Available evidence comes largely from the performance of companies founded by faculty members. Some researchers underscore the role of university venture capital in the formation and success of new companies,[123] while others have found no evidence that university venture capital funding increases the number of university-based start-ups.[124] Nevertheless, university venture capital funds may provide value beyond the capitalizing of new ventures.[125] For student entrepreneurs, they ease the inherent uncertainty of launching a start-up, while signaling its potential to prospective investors and strategic partners. More intangibly, they provide a valuable learning experience to students in handling the actual demands placed on entrepreneurs to meet agreed-upon benchmarks in the company development process.

## Entrepreneurial initiatives in universities

Universities have drawn on the models discussed earlier to support entrepreneurial learning and practice on campus. However, each institution departs from a different position regarding the resources they have available and can access, their local economies, the nature of public policies, and their traditions. While entrepreneurship education courses and programs are generally offered through schools of business and engineering, the home units of extracurricular programs are more varied. It is not uncommon for extracurricular entrepreneurship programs to be self-standing or coordinated from entrepreneurship centers independent of any school. It is also not uncommon for a university's Technology Transfer Office to play a leading role in coordinating university entrepreneurship initiatives, particularly where business and engineering schools do not play that role.[126] At some institutions, entrepreneurship programs are even offered by university housing departments, such as in the case of residential living-learning communities, and even student unions, such as at the University of Western Ontario and Fanshawe College.

Below, four institutions with varying sizes, endowments, and prestige are examined. In spite of these differences, they have emphasized entrepreneurialism as a distinguishing feature that helps them attract students, faculty, and external support. The cases illustrate how the curricular and extracurricular opportunities for students to learn entrepreneurship have taken shape on particular campuses, depicting their often circuitous trajectories as they respond to internal and external drivers.

## Arizona State University

The Arizona State University (ASU) has four campuses in the Phoenix metropolitan area, with nearly 60,200 students on its Tempe campus,[127] making it the largest public university campus in the country. Since becoming ASU President in July 2002, Michael Crow has made entrepreneurship central to vision of growing and transforming the university.[128] By tapping public and private support, the university has dramatically expanded its academic and extracurricular offerings related to entrepreneurship during the last decade.

In this period, the university has promoted faculty and student engagement in start-up activity. In November 2003, the Office of the Vice President for Research and Economic Affairs established Technopolis, a program that offered education, coaching, and networking for technology and life science entrepreneurs in the greater Phoenix area.[129] The program was also opened to faculty and students who were interested in exploring the entrepreneur pathways, but offered little support to student ventures.[130] Until this time, students interested in starting their own business sought council from the College of Business' Center for the Advancement of Small Business. Support for student entrepreneurs gained a boost in 2004 when ASU received $5.4 million by John Edson to establish the Edison Student Entrepreneur Initiative. Students accepted into the program gain support to start and grow a venture.[131] The Edson program also hosts events, such as Demo Days, where ASU student-run companies compete for funding and participate in workshops and networking opportunities, and "Mentor Mashups," were student entrepreneurs' present venture ideas and then mingle with potential mentors.

ASU's technology transfer office has played a significant role in advancing entrepreneurship on campus. Known as Arizona Technology Enterprise,[132] it was created in 2003 as an independent organization so that ASU could own an equity stake in the companies it helps create. Arizona Technology Enterprise is located off-campus at Skysong, a mixed-used business park built in 2008 through collaboration between the City of Scottsdale and the Arizona State University Foundation. In 2010, Arizona Technology Enterprise and the university's research office created a start-up accelerator with financing from federal economic-stimulus funds. Known as Venture Catalyst, the program was open to anyone, and compensated through major milestone payments such as those resulting from an initial public offering, a sale, or significant profits. Venture Catalyst grew to encompass a broad range of entrepreneurship-related activities, and was renamed the Entrepreneurship and Innovation Group (EIG) in 2013.[133]

EIG has made itself the central node of entrepreneurship on campus and the main contact point for the external community. As a site off campus, EIG is a neutral player, not affiliated with any academic unit within the four campuses. The group consolidated a number of programs that had been previously administered by other units. It helps entrepreneurs launch their ventures through programs such as the Edson student Entrepreneur initiative, and the ASU Rapid Startup School, a part-time eight-week program for postdoctoral researchers, graduate students, alumni, and faculty who are interested in venture creation. In addition, the EIG coordinates the Furnace technology transfer accelerator, which provides funding, incubation space, and mentorship to start-ups that license technology and intellectual property from ASU and other participating universities. It recently established the Women's Entrepreneurship Initiative to support female entrepreneurs with support from a grant from the US Small Business Administration.[134]

For students interested in social entrepreneurship, ASU has partnered with the Ashoka Changemaker Campus Consortium and created Changemaker Central, a student-driven initiative that provides a space at each of ASU's campuses for students to become involved in social change through direct service, service learning, and social entrepreneurship.[135] Changemaker Central also houses the Changemaker Challenge, a contest for students with an innovative project, prototype, venture, or community partnership ideas that solve local or global challenges. Another program is 10,000 Solutions, a collaborative online platform where students and community members can submit entrepreneurial solutions to social issues. At the end of the year participants select one submission to receive $10,000 to develop their idea.[136]

To serve students in technological fields, ASU has also partnered with the neighboring City of Chandler and TechShop—a chain of membership-based facilities that provides access to sophisticated tools and equipment—to create the ASU Chandler Innovation Center in downtown Chandler. ASU uses the facility, which is owned by the City of Chandler, to offer a variety of courses in engineering, computing, and product development for students. TechShop operates its TechShop Chandler program in the facility. ASU's College of Technology and Innovation, based at the university's polytechnic campus, offers memberships to students who are taking classes at the center, with discounted memberships available for other students and faculty.[137]

The study of entrepreneurship gained visibility at ASU late in 2006, when the Kauffman Foundation awarded $5 million to the university to support cross-campus entrepreneurship programs for students. At the time, there was some student interest in entrepreneurship, but not a lot of engagement.[138] The university opted not to create a single center of entrepreneurship, believing that multiple centers could have more effect at the large university rather than one single center.

Hence, there has been a multiplication of academic programs in the field. Until the 1990s, entrepreneurship at ASU was contained to a few courses for students within the business school.[139] In 1996, ASU became the first university in the country to offer a minor in Entrepreneurship and Small Business Management open to nonbusiness majors.[140] Today, a number of schools offer entrepreneurship programs. The Center for Entrepreneurship at the W. P. Carey School of Business offers a Bachelor of Science degree in Business Entrepreneurship and undergraduate certificates in Knowledge Entrepreneurship and Innovation (open to all students), and Small Business and Entrepreneurship. They also support an entrepreneurship emphasis in the school's MBA program. The Ira A. Fulton Schools of Engineering offers a Bachelor of Science degree in Technological Entrepreneurship and Management. ASU's School of Film, Dance, and Theatre offers a Bachelor of Arts degree in Digital Culture with a concentration in Technological Entrepreneurship, an undergraduate certificate in Arts Entrepreneurship, and a Master of Fine Arts in Theatre, Arts Entrepreneurship, and Management.[141] Finally, since 2006 the Walter Cronkite School of Journalism has offered entrepreneurship education to journalism students through the digital media entrepreneurship program and the New Media Innovation Lab, where students create digital media products for media companies and other organizations.[142]

These schools have also created opportunities for students to try their hands at venture creation. The Carey School center hosts the Sub Devil Igniter Challenge, where selected students are given a chance to pitch their ideas to win award money to build their ventures. In the Fulton Engineering Ventures program, teams of engineering students develop a business concept for a chance to win funding and mentorship to develop their business concept. The Pave Program in Arts Entrepreneurship operates the Arts Venture Incubator. Students accepted into the Arts Venture Incubator also receive guidance and seed funding. In 2014, the Cronkite School opened the Digital Solutions Lab for community businesses—and those run by students—to receive free help on entrepreneurial projects, websites, and other digital ventures such as mobile app development.[143]

ASU's polytechnic campus in Mesa has created multiple opportunities for students to experience entrepreneurship. Students can choose to live in Startup Village, a residential community that supports student entrepreneurs. Startup Residents are expected to enroll in one of ASU's "MAKE classes", one-unit project-based courses during which students learning about venture design, prototyping, marketing an idea, and launching a venture of innovative idea. Residents of Startup Village are also expected to help facilitate ASU Startup Weekend, as well as participating in supporting entrepreneurial activities on campus.[144] Furthermore, students with ideas for digital products or media-related businesses also may develop their ventures in the Startup Labs, where students can access prototyping equipment free of charge.

The decentralized approach taken at ASU to support entrepreneurship has created a range of offerings for students in different majors and campuses. The university boasts having supported more than 80 student ventures between 2011 and 2014, with a reported survival rate of 90 percent. Students in these ventures have reportedly filed for 18 patents to protect intellectual property associated with their start-ups.[145] Nonetheless, this approach has implied in an ebb and flow of programs whose external support expires and becomes reorganized. The university lacks major new resources to advance its entrepreneurship goals; existing programs can be sustained, but they are not easily expanded or able to reach new audiences. Still, the learning and practice of entrepreneurship became a theme across the university's campuses in a variety of formats.

## Ryerson University

Ryerson University is a young public university located in downtown Toronto. The university was founded as the Ryerson Institute of Technology in 1948, with a mission to train the growing workforce in Ontario's booming postwar economy. In 1964, a provincial bill gave the institution the authority to grant degrees, changing its name to the Ryerson Polytechnical Institute. The Institute gained full university status in 1993, when it established research and graduate programs. In 2001, the school assumed its current name as Ryerson University.[146] A neighbor of the distinguished University of Toronto and York University, Ryerson's transformation from technical institute to university has entailed seizing opportunities to make itself relevant to the needs of the local economy. In line with this trajectory, the university has recently branded itself as "Canada's comprehensive innovation university," and its 2014–2019 academic plan highlights making innovation and entrepreneurship mainstream on campus.[147]

This more recent focus on entrepreneurship emerged in March 2009, when President Sheldon Levy announced his intention to make digital media a top priority for the university.[148] Levy's choice followed the political and economic contexts of the university. At the time, the Ontario government's Innovation Agenda emphasized media and information & communications technologies as a priority for investments. Ontario's entertainment and creative sector, heavily concentrated in Toronto, is the third largest in North America, after California and New York. As a key initiative in this area, the university provided capital for the creation of the Digital Media Zone (DMZ) in April 2010.

DMZ is a space from which to help students and alumni develop marketable digital products and services. Start-ups accepted to the DMZ receive four months of free coworking space and services. After this period they can pay a membership fee to stay on as tenants. Start-ups that are further along in their business development have access to seed funding and an accelerator program through Ryerson Futures Inc. (RFI), a for-profit entity associated with the university. RFI makes selective investments of up to $80,000 in high-potential start-ups. Providing they meet the criteria, start-ups can enter the acceleration program directly upon joining the DMZ. In the few years since it was established, the DMZ has undergone two expansions that have nearly tripled its size. Encompassing 16,400 square feet, the DMZ is one of Canada's largest incubators.[149]

The incubator became a hub of entrepreneurial activity at Ryerson, helping attract external visibility and support. In the words of one faculty member, the DMZ has become the university's "Emerald City," where press conferences are given and public officials are invited for tours. Indeed, the Government of Canada officially designated 2011 as the Year of the Entrepreneur at the DMZ.[150] Also located within the DMZ is the Ryerson Centre for Cloud and Context-Aware Computing, funded by the Federal Economic Development Agency for Southern Ontario. The center supports Southern Ontario companies to develop "context aware" applications for mobile devices.[151] In 2012, the university began offering an optional Digital Specialization Program during which students complete one course in digital economy and then enroll in a 12-week "Digital Specialization Semester" during which students pursue an entrepreneurial idea that has the potential to become operational.

Ryerson's teaching offerings have also been expanded. Entrepreneurship courses at Ryerson University are offered through the business school's Entrepreneurship and Strategy Department, one of the largest entrepreneurship academic departments in Canada. The department houses both a major (for business students) and minor degree program (for nonbusiness majors), 12 faculty members, and over a dozen entrepreneurship courses, many of which are open to students from other degree programs. Entrepreneurship education within the business school is also found in the MBA in Management of Technology and Innovation and MMSc in the Management of Technology and Innovation. In 2013,

Ryerson introduced the Master's in Digital Media, an intensive 12-month professional program.

Much of the momentum for supporting entrepreneurship at the university has come from the efforts of Enactus Ryerson, the student chapter of the nonprofit organization that promotes entrepreneurialism and has chapters at 1,600 universities and colleges worldwide.[152] Enactus Ryerson hosts speakers, participates in regional, national, and international business plan competitions, and since 2001, hosts the Slaight Business Plan Competition on the Ryerson campus. Participating students present their business ideas to a panel of judges for a chance to win $25,000. Under the guidance of Enactus Ryerson's faculty advisor, Enactus students established StartMeUp Ryerson, an initiative for promoting entrepreneurship that offers idea consultation, workshops, and mentorship connections to Ryerson students.[153]

The Provost office has for several years played a coordinating role, allocating relatively modest resources to leverage initiatives such as those of Enactus Ryerson, through the Ryerson Entrepreneurship Institute (REI), created in 2008.[154] REI helps coordinate cross-discipline programs and encourages professors to integrate entrepreneurial content into their courses. The REI has also served as a first-stop for faculty interested in spinning off their research into a new company. In late 2014, REI partnered with the Ted Rogers School of Management to launch the Startup School, a modular learning series to support rising start-ups at the university. Each semester, the Startup School will host 13 different modules focused on helping students grow their start-ups.

Initiatives to foster entrepreneurship on campus continue to flourish across schools and departments. In 2012, with the help donors, the university established an endowed chair in social innovation and entrepreneurship, housed in the Faculty of Community Service's School of Child and Youth Care. To support student experiential learning and entrepreneurship activities, the Faculty of Engineering, Architecture, and Science is developing its Centre for Engineering Innovation and Entrepreneurship. The Norman Esch Engineering Innovation and Entrepreneurship Award competition already provide financial assistance to current engineering and architecture students with promising business ideas. In the Fall of 2013, the university's Student Housing Services formed the Entrepreneurship and Innovation Living Learning Community (LLC), which received the most applications of all campus LLCs.[155] Throughout the year, residents participate in several cocurricular experiences, including various networking opportunities and the "Get Started in Residence" workshop series. Student Housing Services also collaborate with Ryerson Zone Learning on a capstone experience: the inaugural Rye Rez Innovation Challenge. For its inaugural year, the challenge prompted residence students to pitch an innovative solution to improve the experience of commuter students. The winning students were offered support to connect with other entrepreneurs working on similar projects, as well as training and skill development.[156]

Ryerson has successfully made a mark in the Canadian digital entrepreneurship scene with DMZ. The incubator has brought publicity to the rising career-focused institution, and created a "brand" that has been explored in a range of emerging formats discussed earlier.[157] Experiential learning with an entrepreneurial ethos underlies these efforts. Starting in the fall of 2014, the university began new innovation and entrepreneurship "learning zones" based on the concept of the DMZ. "Zone learning" is aligned with Ryerson's mandate to deliver career-relevant education and the ideas of experiential learning guiding entrepreneurship programs. Students may apply to participate in "zones" emphasizing media, fashion, design fabrication, and social ventures, and once admitted are registered in a for-credit course, and are able to access mentoring and relevant project-based learning opportunities. This initiative seeks to blend academic and experiential study through the creation of learning communities.[158]

## University of Southern California

The University of Southern California is a private research university located two miles southwest of downtown Los Angeles. The university has a reputation for having strong support from its alumni. In the university's recent campaign to raise $6 billion by 2018, university alumni have contributed $2.2 billion of $3.7 billion raised so far, making USC one of top fundraising universities in 2013, behind only Stanford and Harvard.[159] The growth of entrepreneurship at USC is attributed in large part by alumni support and expectations that the university become a regional hub for entrepreneurship and innovation.

Entrepreneurship at USC began in the 1960s when the university offered its first course in the topic for graduate students. In 1971, an entrepreneurship course for undergraduates was created, along with a concentration in entrepreneurship at the MBA level that was the first in the United States. In the late 1970s, an undergraduate concentration in entrepreneurship was added, and like the graduate concentration, it was the first of its kind in the country.[160] Near the end of the 1990s, increased interest in entrepreneurship emerged in other academic units.[161] In early 1996, the entrepreneurship program began to serve engineering students who wanted to substitute an entrepreneurship course with a required course in engineering economics. This was the first time that a business course had been approved as part of a degree program in electrical engineering and computer science.

In 1997, MBA in entrepreneurship alumnus Lloyd Greif gave $5 million to the university's business school to establish the Lloyd Greif Center for Entrepreneurial Studies—the first gift of its kind, from an alumnus to a program in this field.[162] As part of the endowment, USC agreed to give the Lloyd Greif Center exclusive rights to the term "entrepreneurship" in titles of courses and programs at the university.[163] A year later, a $100 million donation from entrepreneur Alfred Mann to the school of engineering established the Alfred Mann Institute for Biomedical Engineering to incubate businesses founded on medical devices. The school of engineering and the school of business formed the USC Technology Commercialization Alliance, which intended to serve as a central source of information and coordination regarding research commercialization on campus. In 2004, the USC Technology Commercialization Alliance became the USC Marshall Center for Technology Commercialization. The center provides several entrepreneurial opportunities for students, such as a Certificate in Technology Commercialization, in conjunction with the Lloyd Greif Center for Entrepreneurial Studies. The certificate program pairs MBA students with researchers to create technology/market roadmaps, and connects students with internships through partnership with LA's Business Technology Center and with USC alumni.

In 2004, venture capitalist and USC alumnus Mark Stevens and his wife Mary donated $22 million to the university's school of engineering to create the USC Stevens Institute for Technology Commercialization. The original design for the center was to commercialize faculty technology and to teach students about the commercialization process.[164] In 2006, USC's Office of Technology Licensing—located off campus—was brought under the Institute.[165] A year later the center was re-branded as the USC Stevens Center for Innovation, and took on a university-wide role in fostering innovation under the Office of the Provost.[166] The centralized approach to entrepreneurship education was unsuccessful. The existing programs and centers on campus had already carved several niches into the campus entrepreneurship ecosystem, with each striving to become the authority for entrepreneurship education on campus. Cross-disciplinary collaboration was also thwarted by the university's decentralized approach toward budget management that placed responsibility for financial planning and management at each academic unit. Furthermore, alumni loyal to their home school or department made decentralized fundraising more efficient than a centralized approach. As a result, in 2013, a new executive director returned the center to a focus on supporting technology licensing.[167]

USC continues with a decentralized approach of entrepreneurship programs across schools. Nevertheless, the Lloyd Greif Center for Entrepreneurial Studies has made enrolling nonbusiness students from across campus a primary strategic objective.[168] The center offers five interdisciplinary minors in entrepreneurship, a Masters of Science degree program in entrepreneurship and innovation, and a graduate certificate program in technology commercialization. The center also hosts new venture and business plan competitions, workshops, internships with start-ups, an annual showcase of student entrepreneurs, and an accelerator summer program. It also offers elective courses and concentrations in entrepreneurship and venture management, as well as in technology commercialization to MBA students.[169]

Also within the business school is the Brittingham Social Enterprise Lab, founded as the Society and Business Lab in 2008 with a $1 million commitment from the Salesforce.com (a company founded and led by USC Marshall alumnus Marc Benioff),[170] and $300,000 from the Lord Foundation. The original focus of the Lab was on corporate social responsibility. In 2011, the Lab introduced a social entrepreneurship minor, open to all students, after the Provost at the time expressed an interest in creating a social entrepreneurial program at USC.[171] A $5 million gift from the Brittingham Family Foundation in 2014 advanced new emphasis on social entrepreneurship.[172] The Brittingham Social Enterprise Lab houses the Master of Science in Social Entrepreneurship. Moreover, the lab funds faculty projects integrating business and society both in their teaching and research. A number of other academic and extracurricular offerings are available through the lab, such as undergraduate and graduate courses on social entrepreneurship, internships, and service-learning opportunities, and a variety of events.

Another entrepreneurship education hub on campus is the USC Annenberg Innovation Lab. In 2008, Ernest Wilson became Dean of the

Annenberg School for Journalism and Communication with the aim of making the school an active participant in the broader ecosystem of news and information creation and distribution, much in the same way that schools of medicine, business, or law are integrated with their respective professional environments.¹⁷³ One of the related initiatives was the creation of the Annenberg Innovation Lab in 2010, to support students develop applied projects that respond to the digital media needs of journalists, governments, foundations, and businesses.¹⁷⁴ The lab received a major boost in 2014 in the form of a $3.5-million partnership funded by Blackstone Charitable Foundation, involving UCLA, UC-Irvine, and the Los Angeles County Economic Development Corporation. The Blackstone LaunchPad program provides aspiring entrepreneurs with the tools and supportive mentors they need to launch start-ups. The program LaunchPad is modeled after a successful program developed at the University of Miami in 2008.¹⁷⁵ Finally, Annenberg created an interdisciplinary Media, Economics & Entrepreneurship minor program in partnership with the Lloyd Greif center in 2014.

In 2010, the Massiah Foundation and the USC Viterbi School of Engineering announced a $1-million endowment to fund the creation of the Maseeh Entrepreneurship Prize Competition (MEPC) for the school's engineering students.¹⁷⁶ To assist in launching and managing this endowed program, the school appointed a faculty director of innovation and entrepreneurship.¹⁷⁷ Since 2012, student innovation has been supported through the Viterbi Student Institute for Innovation, formed by a faculty member. The institute also offers new venture creation support and networking opportunities, including the Viterbi Startup Garage—a 12-week technology accelerator program for engineering students.¹⁷⁸ In 2014, NSF awarded a $300,000 grant to the USC I-Corps Site Program to fund start-ups and entrepreneurship among faculty and students. The money will be distributed through the MEPC and the USC iDiploma Certificate Program, an Office of the Provost program for PhD students in science, technology, engineering, and mathematics (STEM) disciplines. Program participants can access NSF grant money to develop translational research project, and the teams with the most outstanding project earn the Diploma in Innovation.¹⁷⁹

In 2013, the university received a $70-million gift to establish the USC Jimmy Iovine and Andre Young Academy for Arts, Technology, and the Business of Innovation. The academy supports a four-year course of study providing academic and experiential learning in three main areas:

art and design, engineering and computer science, and business and venture management.[180] Having admitted its first cohort of 25 students in 2014, the academy has bold aspirations to "instill in its students an entirely new way of thinking" through a multidisciplinary core curriculum, specialized learning involving creative and design skills, and practical experimentation at the "Garage," where students are expected to move from concepts to prototypes.[181] In their senior year, students are immersed in the Garage, a collaborative workspace with prototyping facilities where students work under the guidance of faculty and business mentors. The academy blends elements of hatcheries into an exclusive form of undergraduate multidisciplinary program.

As a leading private university situated in a vibrant regional economy, USC has amassed major resources to build entrepreneurship programs across campus. Attempts at centralizing the operation of entrepreneurship support failed in this context, where strong schools are able to marshal philanthropic support for special initiatives, and leverage other sources of funding. A pioneer in some ways, USC has been expanding the reach of its entrepreneurial initiatives into the classroom and in venture creation.

## University of Waterloo

The University of Waterloo is within its namesake city in Southern Ontario, about 59 miles (113 km) west of Toronto. The university was established in 1957 as the Waterloo College Associate Faculties, a semi-autonomous entity of the then Waterloo College. The associated faculties were composed of science, math, and engineering disciplines, while Waterloo College provided liberal arts and social science education. In 1959, the associated faculties were granted university status, becoming the University of Waterloo.[182] Since then the university has added other disciplines, while retaining its strong reputation in engineering and technological areas. In 2011, the University of Waterloo identified entrepreneurship as one of its six foundation pillars.[183]

The University of Waterloo has a tradition as an entrepreneurial university. The university has contributed to local and regional development by facilitating academic spin-off activity, training and employing skilled graduates at a local level, and developing research excellence in several emerging areas of science and engineering. Indeed, Waterloo's focus on engineering, math, and computer science, in combination with a strong local manufacturing base, helped to form a high-technology cluster in the region.[184] A large number of companies were spun-off of faculty research during the 1970s and 1980s, such as Dantec Electronic, Virtek Vision, and Open Text, and maintained close relations with the university. Blackberry (formerly Research in Motion) is another significant firm in the Waterloo technology ecosystem, but rather than being formed as a result of university-based science, the company was formed by a student who left the university to pursue his own technology projects.[185] The success of these, and other, companies has provided the University of Waterloo and the surrounding region with sources of philanthropy, local reinvestment, and magnets that hire and attract highly skilled workers and other technology-based firms to locate in the region. The university continues to contribute to the development of the regional economy, but the creation of new companies is no longer its main contribution. Since the late 1980s, relatively fewer start-ups have been created from the university.[186]

From its beginning, the University of Waterloo has had close ties with the surrounding business community.[187] The university was formed in the vision of community leaders that called for engineering and technical education that would provide the region with talent and obviate the task of recruiting skilled workers from nearby Toronto. Prominent members of the regional industrial community served as members on the Board of Governors and proposed that education be offered on a cooperative basis with industry. Cooperative education became a defining feature of students' education at the university, with students rotating between the classroom and industry placements. Today, the University of Waterloo runs the largest co-op program in the world, involving 18,300 students (67 percent of the student body) and 5,200 employers each year.[188] After graduation, many students find full-time employment with the firms at which they completed their co-op program.[189] Connections between the university and surrounding firms forged by the co-op programs have also permitted the two to keep abreast of technological developments forged by the other.[190]

Since 2000 the university has emphasized innovation and entrepreneurship education. Soon after being appointed university president in 1999, David Johnston sought to strengthen the university's role in these areas.[191] In 2001, the University launched a not-for-profit company called "UW Innovate Inc.", with support from the Business Development Bank of Canada and the National Research Council, to support pre-incubation innovation and entrepreneurship activities on campus.[192] In 2002, the Waterloo Senate approved the creation of the Centre for

Business, Entrepreneurship and Technology (CBET), which superseded UWInnovate Inc. as the focal point on campus for the university's business activities. The center was largely a response to calls for a formal approach to business education that had been under discussion at the university for several years, as Waterloo has no business school.[193] The Senate also approved the creation of the Master of Business, Entrepreneurship and Technology program, which is housed within the center. Later that year, the administration announced that academic entrepreneurship would become a defining characteristic of Waterloo, in response to the federal government's innovation strategy.[194]

As a standalone center operating on a cost-recovery basis, CBET struggled for a few years as it could not hire faculty and revenue sources were not forthcoming. In 2006 it joined the engineering school and soon after it moved to the Accelerator Building on the North Campus Research and Technology Park, benefiting from a private gift from the Conrad family.[195] In its new space, the center was in closer interaction with start-up organizations in the Accelerator Centre, service providers, and regional entrepreneurs. Thanks to another gift from the Conrads in 2010 the center was renamed after their patrons, becoming the Conrad Centre for Business, Entrepreneurship and Technology. Today, operational funds come from MBET student tuition, course fees from outreach programs, assistance from government-funded technology transfer organizations such as the Ontario Centres for Excellence, and the Dobson Foundation for Entrepreneurship.[196]

The Conrad Center consolidated its role as the hub for entrepreneurship education on campus with multiple offerings, from an undergraduate course on the foundations of venture creation to the Master of Engineering in Business and Entrepreneurship. The center began an entrepreneurship option for engineering students in 2014, and the Bridging Entrepreneurs to Students program places first-year engineering students with seed and early-stage start-up companies as part of co-op placement. Besides, students can use their co-op work term to start their own business through the center. In 2013, the center's founding director was appointed as special advisor, entrepreneurship, to coordinate and plan campus-wide entrepreneurship activities.[197]

Waterloo's Velocity Residence, opened in the fall of 2008 by the university's housing department, was one of Canada's first student business incubators.[198] In addition to 70 single residence rooms, VeloCity has a conference room, a wireless device lab sponsored by Rogers

Communications, and a large collaboration space where students work on their digital media ideas.[199] The Velocity Director is a former Waterloo graduate and Director of Developer Relations at Blackberry. In March 2011, a former VeloCity resident donated $1 million to the university to expand support for student entrepreneurs. The funds inspired the university to establish its own 1 million seed fund for student start-ups.[200]

The success of the VeloCity residence spurred the creation of the VeloCity Garage in February 2012. The VeloCity Garage is a 6,500 square foot space, free for University of Waterloo students and alumni to work in. In the years since, Velocity has grown into a set of six interlinked entrepreneurial initiatives, including Velocity Residence and Velocity Garage, as well as Velocity Alpha (weekly workshops, discussions, and networking events for all students), Velocity Science (an entrepreneurship program focused on biology, chemistry, physics, and earth & environmental sciences), Velocity Foundry (an entrepreneurship program focused on hardware & life sciences start-ups) and the Velocity Fund (which awards grants to selected student ventures). The fund was established with donations from Velocity alumni and a regional angle investor.[201]

Entrepreneurship is also part of Waterloo's satellite campus in the city of Stratford, which is part of the University's Faculty of Arts. The campus, focused on digital media, has been funded by the provincial and federal governments and the Waterloo-based software company Open Text—a spin-off of Waterloo and Canada's largest software company. The campus leads the Canadian Digital Media Network. Engage Lab is an experiential learning setting on the Stratford campus, a digital media "sandbox" equipped with technology to encourage research, experimentation, and prototype development and commercialization. The Stratford Accelerator Centre, which helps early-stage technology and digital media companies in the city of Stratford, will be relocating to the Waterloo Stratford Campus in 2015.[202]

Initiatives to support entrepreneurial education and practice continue to flourish at Waterloo. The next development at the university will be the construction of the Engineering Entrepreneurship Building (E7), which will house programs to foster collaboration and entrepreneurship.[203] The building will contain several work spaces, such as a student machine shop, an electronics components shop, designed to support undergraduate experiential learning and prototype development.[204] The university prides itself on being an "entrepreneurial" university, and derives much of its reputation from the record it established in this area.

\* \* \*

The diffusion of entrepreneurship concentrations, majors, minors, and other degree equivalents across universities suggest the maturation of the field. Dedicated courses, endowed positions, degree programs, and research centers denote the heightened status of entrepreneurship in higher education. While advocates continue to experience cultural and organizational challenges to entrepreneurship research and education on campuses, as well as a lack of support for initiatives outside of the main academic functions of universities,[205] entrepreneurship programming has multiplied inside and outside the classroom. Moreover, it counts on considerable external support from philanthropy, governments, and the business community. Public and private funding, as well as campus resources are devoted to the sprawling web of support units and programs that promote and facilitate the creation of start-ups on campus.

Less tangible, but no less important to the embedding of entrepreneurship education into colleges and universities, is the social cache currently enjoyed by entrepreneurs. Positive reflections of entrepreneurs in the media and popular culture shine a bright light on university initiatives aimed at cultivating entrepreneurialism. Even though its place in higher education might be a matter of internal debate, external depictions of university student entrepreneurship initiatives are usually favorable, if not laudatory. That indeed is the general perception of the public when asked about how the media depicts entrepreneurs in general.[206] Considering the strong orientation at universities toward maintaining a positive public image as a means of bolstering legitimacy and prestige, the current status of entrepreneurship is a powerful incentive for further advancement of this field in higher education.

# Notes

1  Robert Ronstadt, "The Educated Entrepreneurs: A New Era of Entrepreneurial Education Is Beginning," *American Journal of Small Business* 10, no. 1 (1985): 7–23.

2   Karl H. Vesper and William Gartner, "Measuring Progress in Entrepreneurship Education," *Journal of Business Venturing* 12 (1997): 403–421; Jerome A. Katz, "The Chronology and Intellectual Trajectory of American Entrepreneurship Education: 1876–1999," *Journal of Business Venturing* 18, no. 2 (2003): 283–300; Donald F. Kuratko, "The Emergence of Entrepreneurship Education: Development, Trends, and Challenges," *Entrepreneurship Theory and Practice* 29, no. 5 (2005): 577–598.

3   Katz, "The Chronology and Intellectual Trajectory of American Entrepreneurship Education: 1876–1999."

4   Karl H. Vesper and W. Ed McMullan, "Entrepreneurship: Today Courses, Tomorrow Degrees?" *Entrepreneurship Theory and Policy* 13, no. 1 (1988): 7–13; Gerald E. Hills, "Variations in University Entrepreneurship Education: An Empirical Study of An Evolving Field," *Journal of Business Venturing* 3, no. 2 (1988): 109–122.

5   Jerome A. Katz, "Fully Mature but Not Fully Legitimate: A Different Perspective on the State of Entrepreneurship Education," *Journal of Small Business Management* 46, no. 4 (2008): 550–566; This estimation includes small business courses, and follows Solomon, Duffy, and Tarabishy's estimate that the number of entrepreneurship *and* small business education classes in higher education (within business schools) at around 1,200 in the United States (see George T. Solomon, Susan Duffy, and Ayman Tarabishy, "The State of Entrepreneurship Education in the United States: A Nationwide Survey and Analysis," *International Journal of Entrepreneurship Education* 1, no. 1 (2002): 65–86). Katz offers an estimation of the number of entrepreneurship courses offered at college and universities throughout the United States at over 500 (see Katz, "The Chronology and Intellectual Trajectory of American Entrepreneurship Education: 1876–1999").

6   National Association for Community College Entrepreneurship, *About NACCE* (2010), accessed March 4, 2014, http://www.nacce.com/?Introduction.

7   Elizabeth Hagan, *Entrepreneurship Education: A New Frontier for American Community Colleges* (PhD diss., Union Institute and University, 2004).

8   Teresa V. Menzies, *Entrepreneurship and the Canadian University* (St. Catharines, ON: Brock University, 2004).

9   Teresa V. Menzies, *Entrepreneurship and the Canadian Universities: Strategies and Best Practices of Entrepreneurship Centres* (Faculty of Business, Brock University; John Dobson Foundation, 2009); Industry Canada, *The Teaching and Practice of Entrepreneurship within Canadian Higher Education Institutions* (Ottawa, ON: Industry Canada, 2010).

10  Kuratko, "The Emergence of Entrepreneurship Education: Development, Trends, and Challenges."

11. W. Ed McMullan and Wayne A Long, "Entrepreneurship Education in the Nineties," *Journal of Business Venturing* 2, no. 3 (1987): 261–275.
12. Heidi M. Neck and Patricia G. Greene, "Entrepreneurship Education: Known Worlds and New Frontiers," *Journal of Small Business Management* 49, no. 1 (2011): 55–70; Sascha G. Walter and Dirk Dohse, "Why Mode and Regional Context Matter for Entrepreneurship Education," *Entrepreneurship & Regional Development* 24, no. 9–10 (2012): 807–835; Steve Blank, "Why the Lean Start-up Changes Everything," *Harvard Business Review* 91, no. 5 (2013): 63–72.
13. David A. Kirby, "Entrepreneurship Education: Can Business Schools Meet the Challenge?" *Education + Training* 46, no. 8/9 (2004): 510–519; Vangelis Souitaris, Stefania Zerbinati, and Andreas Al-Laham, "Do Entrepreneurship Programmes Raise Entrepreneurial Intention of Science and Engineering Students? The Effect of Learning, Inspiration and Resources," *Journal of Business Venturing* 22, no. 4 (2007): 566–591.
14. Charles D. Davis, Gerald E. Hills, and Raymond W. LaForge, "The Marketing/Small Enterprise Paradox: A Research Agenda," *International Small Business Journal* 3, no. 3 (1985): 31–42; Ronstadt, "The Educated Entrepreneurs: A New Era of Entrepreneurial Education Is Beginning."
15. Vesper and McMullan, "Entrepreneurship: Today Courses, Tomorrow Degrees?"; William B. Gartner and Karl Vesper, "Experiments in Entrepreneurship Education: Success and Failures," *Journal of Business Venturing* 9 (1994): 179–187.
16. Donald F. Kuratko, *Entrepreneurship: Theory, Process, Practice* (Mason, OH: South-Western, 2014), 3.
17. William B. Gartner, "What Are We Talking About When We Talk About Entrepreneurship?" *Journal of Business Venturing* 5, no. 1 (1990): 15–28; Luke Pittaway, "Philosophies in Entrepreneurship: A Focus on Economic Theories," *International Journal of Entrepreneurial Behaviour & Research* 11, no. 3 (2005): 201–221; Kuratko, *Entrepreneurship: Theory, Process, Practice*; Allan O'Connor, "A Conceptual Framework for Entrepreneurship Education Policy: Meeting Government and Economic Purposes," *Journal of Business Venturing* 28, no. 4 (2013): 546–563.
18. George Solomon, "An Examination of Entrepreneurship Education in the United States, *Journal of Small Business and Enterprise Development* 14, no 2. (2008): 168–182.
19. Katz, "Fully Mature but Not Fully Legitimate: A Different Perspective on the State of Entrepreneurship Education."
20. McMullan and Long, "Entrepreneurship Education in the Nineties."
21. Michael H. Morris, Donald F. Kuratko, and Jeffrey R. Cornwall, *Entrepreneurship Programs and the Modern University* (Cheltenham, UK: Edward Elgar Publishing, 2013).
22. Teresa V. Menzies, *Entrepreneurship and the Canadian University*; Todd A. Finkle, Donald F. Kuratko, and Michael G. Goldsby, "An Examination of

Entrepreneurship Centers in the United States: A National Survey," *Journal of Small Business Management* 44, no. 2 (2006): 184–206; Solomon, "An Examination of Entrepreneurship Education in the United States."

23  Morris, Kuratko, and Cornwall, *Entrepreneurship Programs and the Modern University*; Creso Sá, Andrew Kretz, and Kristjan Sigurdson, *The State of Entrepreneurship Education in Ontario's Colleges and Universities* (Ontario: Higher Education Quality Council of Ontario, 2014).

24  Hills, "Variations in University Entrepreneurship Education: An Empirical Study of an Evolving Field"; Solomon, "An Examination of Entrepreneurship Education in the United States."

25  Hills, "Variations in University Entrepreneurship Education: An Empirical Study of An Evolving Field"; Lawrence A. Klatt, "A Study of Small Business/ entrepreneurial Education in Colleges and Universities," *The Journal of Private Enterprise* 4 (1988): 103–108; Vesper and McMullan, "Entrepreneurship: Today Courses, Tomorrow Degrees?"; Calven A. Kent, "Entrepreneurship Education at the Collegiate Level: A Synopsis and Evaluation," in *Entrepreneurship Education: Current Developments, Future Directions*, ed. Calven A. Kent (Westport, CT: Quorum Books, 1990); Gartner and Vesper, "Experiments in Entrepreneurship Education: Success and Failures." Gary Gorman, Dennis Hanlon, and Wayne King, "Some Research Perspectives on Entrepreneurship Education, Enterprise Education and Education for Small Business Management: A Ten-year Literature Review," *International Small Business Journal* 15, no. 3 (1997): 56–76; Benson Honig, "Entrepreneurship Education: Toward a Model of Contingency-based Business Planning," *Academy of Management Learning & Education* 3, no. 3 (2004): 258–273; Solomon, "An Examination of Entrepreneurship Education in the United States."

26  Jerome A. Katz and Richard P. Green, *Entrepreneurial Small Business* (McGraw-Hill/Irwin, 2007); Morris, Kuratko and Cornwall, *Entrepreneurship Programs and the Modern University*.

27  Kauffman Foundation, *The Growth and Advancement of Entrepreneurship in Higher Education: An Environmental Scan of College Initiatives* (Kauffman Center for Entrepreneurial Leadership, Kansas City, MO, 2001); Anita Leffel and Cory R. A. Hallam, "Stimulating Entrepreneurial Enterprise Development: Business Plan Competitions Are Not the Answer," in the *Association for Small Business & Entrepreneurship 35th Annual Conference Proceedings* (2008): 162–188; Linda W. Ross and Kimble A. Byrd, "Business Plan Competitions: Start-up 'Idols' and Their Twenty-First Century Launch Pads," *Journal of Higher Education Theory and Practice* 11, no. 4 (2011): 53–64.

28  Katz, "The Chronology and Intellectual Trajectory of American Entrepreneurship Education: 1876–1999."

29  Kauffman Foundation, *The Growth and Advancement of Entrepreneurship in Higher Education: An Environmental Scan of College Initiatives*.

30 Leffel and Hallam, "Stimulating Entrepreneurial Enterprise Development: Business Plan Competitions Are Not the Answer."
31 "Entrepreneurship: Student Competitions," *Faculty of Engineering, University of Ottawa*, accessed November 1, 2014, http://engineering.uottawa.ca/entrepreneurship/student-competitions.
32 Ibid.
33 In addition to the School of Business's Lloyd Greif Center for Entrepreneurship Studies' New Venture Seed Competition, which is open to all students, and the Maseeh Entrepreneurship Prize Competition, which is intended for engineering students. See "Venture Competitions," *Lloyd Greif Center for Entrepreneurial Studies, Marshall School of Business, University of Southern* California, accessed November 1, 2014, http://www.marshall.usc.edu/faculty/centers/greif/programs/usc-competitions.
34 Teresa V. Menzies, "An Exploratory Study of University Entrepreneurship Centers in Canada," *Journal of Small Business and Entrepreneurship* 15, no. 3 (2000): 15–38; Kauffman Foundation, *The Growth and Advancement of Entrepreneurship in Higher Education: An Environmental Scan of College Initiatives*.
35 Alberta Charney, Gary D. Libecap, and Karl Eller Center, *The Impact of Entrepreneurship Education: An Evaluation of the Berger Entrepreneurship Program at the University of Arizona* (Tucson, Arizona: The Karl Eller Center of The College of Business and Public Administration, 2000); Katz, "The Chronology and Intellectual Trajectory of American Entrepreneurship Education: 1876—1999"; Todd A. Finkle, Teresa A. Menzies, Donald F. Kuratko, and Michael G. Goldsby, "Financial Activities of Entrepreneurship Centers in the United States," *Journal of Business and Entrepreneurship* 23, no. 2 (2012): 48–64.
36 Menzies, *Entrepreneurship and the Canadian Universities: Strategies and Best Practices of Entrepreneurship Centres*.
37 Finkle, Kuratko, and Goldsby, "An Examination of Entrepreneurship Centers in the United States: A National Survey"; Menzies, "An Exploratory Study of University Entrepreneurship Centers in Canada"; Menzies, *Entrepreneurship and the Canadian Universities: Strategies and Best Practices of Entrepreneurship Centres*.
38 "About the OSU Entrepreneurship Program," *School of Entrepreneurship, Oklahoma State University*, accessed December 1, 2014, http://entrepreneurship.okstate.edu/aboutus/; Michael H. Morris and Donald F. Kuratko, "Building University 21st Century Entrepreneurship Programs That Empower and Transform," in *Innovative Pathways for University Entrepreneurship in the 21st Century*, eds. Donald F. Kuratko and Sherry Loskinson (Bingley, UK: Emerald Group Publishing Limited, 2014), 1–24.
39 Kris Bevill, "Higher Education: Elevating Entrepreneurship," *Prairie Business Magazine*, July 25, 2014, http://www.prairiebizmag.com/event/

article/id/20120/; Niki Glanakaris, "Drexel Establishes Close School of Entrepreneurship, *Drexel Now*, January 30, 2013, accessed October 14, 2014, http://drexel.edu/now/archive/2013/January/Close-School-of-Entrepreneurship/; Morris, Kuratko, and Cornwall, *Entrepreneurship Programs and the Modern University*.

40 Entrepreneurship clubs are student-led organizations that "attract students who are interested in learning about enterprise and developing enterprising skills to either start their own businesses or to become more enterprising people" [Luke Pittaway, Elena Rodriguez-Falcon, Olaojo Aiyegbayo, and Amanda King, "The Role of Entrepreneurship Clubs and Societies in Entrepreneurial Learning," *International Small Business Journal* 29, no. 1 (2011): 39]. These clubs can be either "self-organized" or "sponsored." According to Luke Pittaway, Jim Gazzard, Adam Shore, and Tom Williamson, "self-organized clubs are those formed by students following their own interests while sponsored clubs are mediated by external organizations supporting a particular form of practice," while self-organized clubs are typically independent and usually associated with their campus's student body (i.e., a university's student union), sponsored clubs are part of a larger network of student-based groups [Luke Pittaway, Jim Gazzard, Adam Shore, and Tom Williamson, "Entrepreneurial Learning Through Experience: The Hidden Role of Student Clubs in Management Education," *Center for Entrepreneurial Learning and Leadership* (2012): 6].

41 Justin T. Brown and Andrew C. Kant, "Creating Bioentrepreneurs: How Graduate Student Organisations Foster Science Entrepreneurship," *Journal of Commercial Biotechnology* 15, no. 2 (2009): 125–135; Pittaway et al., "The Role of Entrepreneurship Clubs and Societies in Entrepreneurial Learning"; Pittaway et al., "Entrepreneurial Learning Through Experience: The Hidden Role of Student Clubs in Management Education."

42 Morris, Kuratko, and Cornwall, *Entrepreneurship Programs and the Modern University*.

43 *United States Association for Small Business and Entrepreneurship*, accessed November 10, 2014, http://www.usasbe.org/?

44 "Entrepreneurship Education Awards," *United States Association for Small Business and Entrepreneurship*, accessed November 10, 2014, http://www.usasbe.org/?page=EENawards.

45 "GCEC Awards," *Johnson Center for Entrepreneurship & Innovation Kelley School of Business, Indiana University—Bloomington,* accessed November 10, 2014, http://www.globalentrepreneurshipconsortium.org/GCECawards.cfm.

46 *Kern Entrepreneurial Engineering Network (KEEN)*, accessed November 10, 2014, http://www.keennetwork.org.

47 Deborah H. Streeter and John P. Jaquette Jr, "University-wide Entrepreneurship Education: Alternative Models and Current Trend,"

*The Southern Rural Sociological Association* 20, no. 2 (2004): 44–71; Morris, Kuratko, and Cornwall, *Entrepreneurship Programs and the Modern University*.

48  Streeter and Jaquette Jr, "University-wide Entrepreneurship Education: Alternative Models and Current Trend." In Canada, half of universities and colleges surveyed by Industry Canada in 2009 aim to foster entrepreneurial behaviors, skills, and mindsets, while 23 percent have an institution-wide strategy to deliver entrepreneurship education (Industry Canada, *The Teaching and Practice of Entrepreneurship within Canadian Higher Education Institutions*).

49  Hanns C. Menzel, Iiris Aaltio, and Jan M. Ulijn, "On the Way to Creativity: Engineers as Intrapreneurs in Organizations," *Technovation* 27, no. 12 (2007): 732–743.

50  G. Page West, Elizabeth J. Gatewood, and Kelly G. Shaver, *Handbook of University-wide Entrepreneurship Education* (Cheltenham, UK: Edward Elgar Publishing, 2009); Angela Shartrand, Phil Weilerstein, Mary Besterfield-Sacre, and Katharine Golding, "Technology Entrepreneurship Programs in US Engineering Schools: Course and Program Characteristics at the Undergraduate Level," in *Conference Proceedings: American Society for Engineering Education* (2010).

51  Jerome Katz, *2004 Survey of Endowed Positions in Entrepreneurship and Related Fields in the United States* (Kansas City, MO: Ewing Marion Kauffman Foundation, 2004).

52  "The Coleman Foundation Faculty Entrepreneurship Fellows Program," *The Coleman Foundation*, accessed November 10, 2014, http://www.colemanfoundation.org/what_we_fund/entrepreneurship/fellows.html.

53  Formerly the National Collegiate Inventors and Innovators Alliance (NCIIA).

54  *AshokaU*, accessed October 4, 2014, http://ashokau.org.

55  Matthew M. Mars, "The Diverse Agendas of Faculty within an Institutionalized Model of Entrepreneurship Education," *Journal of Entrepreneurship Education* 10, no. 1 (2007): 43–62.

56  J. Gregory Dees, *The Meaning of "Social Entrepreneurship*," reformatted and revised May 30, 2001, http://www.caseatduke.org/documents/dees_sedef.pdf; Kelly G. Shaver, "Reflections on a New Academic Path: Entrepreneurship in the Arts and Sciences," *Peer Review* 7, no. 3 (2005): 21–23; Jed C. Macosko, A. Daniel Johnson, and Sarah M. Yocum, "Teaching Entrepreneurship Through Science-oriented Teams and Projects: Three Case Studies," in *Handbook of University-wide Entrepreneurship Education*, eds. G. Page West, Elizabeth J. Gatewood, and Kelly G. Shaver (Cheltenham, UK: Edward Elgar Publishing, 2009), 122–135; West, Gatewood and Shaver, *Handbook of University-wide Entrepreneurship Education*.

57  Samuel Hines, "The Practical Side of Liberal Education: An Overview of Liberal Education and Entrepreneurship," *Peer Review* 7, no. 3 (2005):

4–7; Matthew M. Mars, "The Diverse Agendas of Faculty within An Institutionalized Model of Entrepreneurship Education," *Journal of Entrepreneurship Education* 10, no. 1 (2007): 43–62.
58  Joseph Roberts, "Infusing Entrepreneurship within Non-business Disciplines: Preparing Artists and Others for Self-employment and Entrepreneurship," *Artivate: A journal of entrepreneurship in the arts* 1, no. 2 (2013): 53–63.
59  Ibid.
60  Ibid.
61  Gary D. Beckman and Linda Essig, "Arts Entrepreneurship: A Conversation," *Artivate: A journal of entrepreneurship in the arts* 1, no. 1 (2012): 1–8.
62  Dennis Ray, "Liberal Arts for Entrepreneurs", *Entrepreneurship Theory & Practice* 15, no. 2 (1990): 79–93; Shaver, "Reflections on a New Academic Path: Entrepreneurship in the Arts and Sciences"; Mary Godwyn, "Can the Liberal Arts and Entrepreneurship Work Together?" *Academe* 95, no. 1 (2009): 36–38; Dan Edelstein, "How Is Innovation Taught? On the Humanities and the Knowledge Economy," *Liberal Education* 96, no. 1 (2010): 14–19.
63  Hines, "The Practical Side of Liberal Education: An Overview of Liberal Education and Entrepreneurship," 225.
64  Godwyn, "Can the Liberal Arts and Entrepreneurship Work Together?" 37.
65  Matthew D. Regele and Heidi M. Neck, "The Entrepreneurship Education Sub-ecosystem in the United States: Opportunities to Increase Entrepreneurial Activity," *Journal of Business & Entrepreneurship* Winter (2012): 25–47.
66  Hines, "The Practical Side of Liberal Education: An Overview of Liberal Education and Entrepreneurship," 6.
67  Henry G. Rennie, "Entrepreneurship as a Liberal Art," *Politics & Policy* 36, no. 2 (2008): 197–215.
68  Idee Winfield, "Fostering Social Entrepreneurship through Liberal Learning in the Social Sciences," *Peer Review*, no. Spring (2005): 15–17.
69  Eleanor Shaw and Sara Carter, "Social Entrepreneurship: Theoretical Antecedents and Empirical Analysis of Entrepreneurial Processes and Outcomes," *Journal of Small Business and Enterprise Development* 14, no. 3 (2007): 418–434.
70  J. Gregory Dees, *The Meaning of "Social Entrepreneurship"*; Roger L. Martin and Sally Osberg, "Social Entrepreneurship: The Case For Definition," *Sanford Social Innovation Review*, Spring (2007): 29–39; Alex Nicholls, "Introduction," in *Social Entrepreneurship: New Models of Sustainable Change*, ed. Alex Nicholls (Oxford: Oxford University Press, 2010), 1–35.
71  Sage Publications, *SAGE Brief Guide to Corporate Social Responsibility* (Thousand Oaks, CA: Sage Publications, Inc, 2012); Ana Maria Peredo and Murdith McLean, "Social Entrepreneurship: A Critical Review of the Concept," *Journal of World Business* 41, no. 1 (2006): 56–65.

72  Jeremy C. Short, Todd W. Moss and G. T. Lumpkin, "Research in Social Entrepreneurship: Past Contributions and Future Opportunities," *Strategic Entrepreneurship Journal* 3, no. 2 (2009): 161–194; Kristin Joos and Michele Leaman, "Teaching Social Entrepreneurship," in *Annals of Entrepreneurship Education and Pedagogy*, ed. Michael H. Morris (Cheltenham, UK: Edward Elgar Publishers, 2014), 152–173.
73  Debbie D. Brock and Susan D. Steiner, "Social Entrepreneurship Education: Is It Achieving the Desired Aims?" *United States Association for Small Business and Entrepreneurship (USASBE) Conference Proceedings 2008*, February 19, 2009, http://ssrn.com/abstract=1344419.
74  Kristin and Leaman, "Teaching Social Entrepreneurship."
75  Matthew M. Mars, *The Emerging Domains of Entrepreneurship Education: Students, Faculty, and the Capitalist Academy* (PhD diss., University of Arizona, 2006).
76  Debbie D. Brock, *Social Entrepreneurship Education Resource Handbook* (Arlington, VA: Ashoka U, 2011).
77  Kristin and Leaman, "Teaching Social Entrepreneurship."
78  Kirby, "Entrepreneurship Education: Can Business Schools Meet the Challenge?"
79  W. Ed McMullan and Wayne A Long, "Entrepreneurship Education in the Nineties," *Journal of Business Venturing* 2, no. 3 (1987): 261–275; Vesper and McMullan "Entrepreneurship: Today Courses, Tomorrow Degrees?"; Thomas N. Garavan and Barra O'Cinneide, "Entrepreneurship Education and Training Programmes: A Review and Evaluation-Part 1," *Journal of European Industrial Training* 18, no. 8 (1994): 3–12.
80  Morris, Kuratko, and Cornwall, *Entrepreneurship Programs and the Modern University*.
81  Blank, "Why the Lean Start-up Changes Everything," 66.
82  Alexander Osterwalder and Yves Pigneur, *Business Model Generation: A Handbook for Visionaries, Game Changers, and Challengers* (Hoboken, NJ: Wiley, 2010).
83  Eric Ries, *The Lean Startup: How Today's Entrepreneurs Use Continuous Innovation to Create Radically Successful Businesses* (New York: Crown Publishing, 2011).
84  Entrepreneurship educator, Steve Blank, makes an argument for this transformation. See Steve Blank, "No One Wins in Business Plan Competitions," *Steve Blank*, May 17, 2010, accessed October 4, 2014, http://steveblank.com/2010/05/17/no-one-wins-in-business-plan-competitions/; Blank, "Why the Lean Startup Changes Everything."
85  Morris, Kuratko, and Cornwall, *Entrepreneurship Programs and the Modern University*, 160.
86  "Lavin Center Programs," *Lavin Entrepreneurship Center, College of Business Administration*, accessed November 20, 2014, http://lavincenter.sdsu.edu.

87  Jennifer Bechtel, *Building an Entrepreneurial Living-Learning Community* (Innovation Living-Learning Community, University of Illinois Urbana-Champaign), accessed November 10, 2014, http://illinois.edu/cms/1531/llc_manual.pdf.

88  Gary R. Pike, "The Effects of Residential Learning Communities and Traditional Living Arrangements on Educational Gains during the First Year of College," *Journal of College Student Development* 40, no. 3 (1999): 269–284.

89  James Green, "Designing and Launching the Entrepreneurship and Innovation Living-Learning Program for Freshman and Sophomores," *American Society for Engineering Education* (2010), accessed September 14, 2014, http://search.asee.org/search/fetch;jsessionid=79cul1mgefrj4?url=file%3A%2F%2Flocalhost%2FE%3A%2Fsearch%2Fconference%2F32%2FAC%252020 10Full413.pdf&index=conference_papers&space=129746797203605791716676178&type=application%2Fpdf&charset=.

90  *Innovation Square at the University of Florida* (University of Florida Development Corporation), accessed December 1, 2014, http://innovationsquare.ufl.edu/system/files/1_1790163934_uof-11003-innova_sq_broch(m).pdf.

91  "Summer Abroad – Nice, France," *University of California, Berkeley*, accessed December 1, 2014, http://studyabroad.berkeley.edu/berkeleyabroad/nice.

92  "Global and Experiential Programs," Purdue University, accessed December 1, 2014, http://www.purdue.edu/discoverypark/entr/academics/global%20and%20experiential%20programs.php; "Study Abroad," Baylor University, accessed December 1, 2014, http://www.baylor.edu/business/entrepreneurship/index.php?id=89475.

93  "UConn Social Entrepreneur Corps Summer in Guatemala," *University of Connecticut*, accessed on September 28, 2014. http://abroad.uconn.edu/program/uconn-social-entrepreneur-corps-in-guatemala-faculty-led-summer/.

94  *StartupWeekend*, accessed December 1, 2014, http://startupweekend.org.

95  Quentin Casey, "Queen's University Students Organized Startup Summit to Improve Peers' Career Prospects," *Financial Post*, February 27, 2014, accessed March 8, 2014, http://business.financialpost.com/2014/02/27/queens-university-students-organize-startup-summit-to-improve-peers-career-prospects/#__federated=1.

96  Isabel Henderson, *The Princeton Entrepreneurship Club*, November, 20, 2012, accessed November, 19, 2014, http://www.princeton.edu/research/invention/archive/archive/?id=8963.

97  John Duhring, "Project-Based Learning Kickstart Tips: Hackathon Pedagogies as Educational Technology" paper presented at the *National Collegiate Inventors And Innovators Alliance 18th annual Conference* (March 21–22, San Jose, CA, 2014), accessed December 1, 2014, http://nciia.org/open/wp-content/uploads/2013/10/DUHRING.pdf.

98 Calvin Alagot, "UCLA Hosts "Biggest Hackathon in History," *LA Weekly*, April 12, 2014, accessed December 1, 2014, http://www.laweekly.com/informer/2014/04/12/ucla-hosts-biggest-hackathon-in-history.

99 Ben Lutz, Cory Hixson, Marie C. Paretti, Alex Epstein, and Jack Lesko, "Mentoring and Facilitation in Entrepreneurship Education: Beliefs and Practices," paper presented at the *National Collegiate Inventors And Innovators Alliance 18th annual Conference* (March 21–22, San Jose, CA, 2014), accessed October 1, 2014, http://venturewell.org/open2014/wp-content/uploads/2013/10/PARETTI.pdf.

100 Morris, Kuratko, and Cornwall, *Entrepreneurship Programs and the Modern University*.

101 *VentureWell*, accessed December 20, 2014, http://venturewell.org.

102 *Collegiate Entrepreneurs' Organization*, accessed December 20, 2014, http://www.c-e-o.org.

103 Morris, Kuratko, and Cornwall, *Entrepreneurship Programs and the Modern University*.

104 Sean M. Hackett and David M. Dilts, "A Systematic Review of Business Incubation Research," *The Journal of Technology Transfer* 29, no. 1 (2004): 55–82.

105 Creso Sá and Hana Lee, "Science, Business, and Innovation: Understanding Networks in Technology-based Incubators," *R&D Management* 42, no. 3 (2012): 243–253; Susan Cohen and Yael V. Hochberg, *Accelerating Startups: The Seed Accelerator Phenomenon* (March 30, 2014), accessed November 19, 2014, http://ssrn.com/abstract=2418000; Paul Miller and Kirsten Bound, *The Startup Factories: The Rise of Accelerator Programmes to Support New Technology Ventures* (NESTA, June 2011), accessed June 4, 2014, http://www.nesta.org.uk/sites/default/files/the_startup_factories_0.pdf.

106 Kauffman Foundation, *Entrepreneurship Education Comes of Age on Campus* (Ewing Marion Kauffman Foundation, Kansas City: MO, 2013).

107 Ibid., 5.

108 "Velocity," *University of Waterloo*, accessed December 1, 2014, http://velocity.uwaterloo.ca.

109 Linda Essig, "Ownership, Failure, and Experience: Goals and Evaluation Metrics of University-Based Arts Venture Incubators," *Entrepreneurship Research Journal* 4, no. 1 (2014): 117–135.

110 Linda Essig, "Arts Incubators: 47 and Counting," *Creative Infrastructure*, June 26, 2013, accessed October 10, 2013, http://creativeinfrastructure.org/2013/06/26/arts-incubators-47-and-counting/.

111 "Take It To Market Incubator," *OCAD University*, accessed December 1, 2014, http://www.ocadu.ca/research/imagination-catalyst/take-it-to-market.htm.

112 Morris, Kuratko, and Cornwall, *Entrepreneurship Programs and the Modern University*.

113 "UIC Chancellor's Innovation Fund Proof of Concept Award Programs," *Office of Technology Management, University of Illinois at Chicago*, accessed December 10, 2014, http://otm.uic.edu/node/5075.

114 Billy Gallagher, "Stanford University is Going to Invest in Student Startups Like a VC Firm," *TechCrunch*, September 4, 2013, accessed October 5, 2014, http://techcrunch.com/2013/09/04/stanford-university-is-going-to-invest-in-student-startups-like-a-vc-firm/.

115 Heather Somerville, "UC Proposes $250 Million Venture Fund for Faculty-and Student-Led Startups, *SiliconBeat*, September 16, 2014, accessed September 17, 2014, http://www.siliconbeat.com/2014/09/16/uc-proposes-250-million-venture-fund-for-faculty-and-studet-led-startups/.

116 Heather L. Traeger, Theodore W. Kassinger, and Zachary D. Kaufman, "Democratizing Entrepreneurship. An Overview of the Past, Present, and Future of Crowdfunding," *Securities, Regulation and Law Report: BNA Insights* 45, no. 5 (2013): 208–217; Ethan Mollick, "The Dynamics of Crowdfunding: An Exploratory Study," *Journal of Business Venturing* 29, no. 1 (2014): 1–16.

117 Traeger, Kassinger, and Kaufman, "Democratizing Entrepreneurship: An Overview of the Past, Present, and Future of Crowdfunding"; Mollick, "The Dynamics of Crowdfunding: An Exploratory Study."

118 Christopher-John Cornell, "Crowdfunding: More Than Money Jumpstarting University Entrepreneurship," paper presented at the *National Collegiate Inventors And Innovators Alliance 18th annual Conference* (March 21–22, San Jose, CA, 2014), accessed December 30, 2014, http://venturewell.org/open2014/wp-content/uploads/2013/10/CORNELL-2.pdf.

119 "Tech Debuts New Crowd-Funding Website," *Georgia Institute of Technology*, May 13, 2013, accessed September 4, 2014, http://www.news.gatech.edu/2013/05/13/tech-debuts-new-crowd-funding-website.

120 "Crowdfunding on College Campuses," *Launcht*, October 25, 2012, accessed November 20, 2014, http://www.launcht.com/blog/2012/10/25/crowdfunding-on-college-campuses/.

121 Cornell, "Crowdfunding: More Than Money Jumpstarting University Entrepreneurship."

122 "Georgetown Startup Stipend Program," *Georgetown University*, accessed November 14, 2014, http://startuphoyas.com/stipend/.

123 Annalisa Croce, Luca Grilli, and Samuele Murtinu, "Venture Capital Enters Academia: An Analysis of University-managed Funds," *The Journal of Technology Transfer* 39, no. 5 (2013): 1–28.

124 Dante Di Gregorio and Scott Shane, "Why Do Some Universities Generate More Start-ups Than Others?" *Research Policy* 32, no. 2 (2003): 209–227.

125 Josh Lerner, "The University and the Start-up: Lessons from the Past Two Decades," *The Journal of Technology Transfer* 30, no. 1–2 (2004): 49–56.

124   *The Entrepreneurship Movement and the University*

126   Menzies, *Entrepreneurship and the Canadian Universities: Strategies and Best Practices of Entrepreneurship Centres*; Morris, Kuratko, and Cornwall, *Entrepreneurship Programs and the Modern University*; Sá, Kretz and Sigurdson, *The State of Entrepreneurship Education In Ontario's Colleges and Universities*; Streeter and Jaquette Jr, "University-wide Entrepreneurship Education: Alternative Models and Current Trend"; Confidential interview by Andrew Kretz, Los Angeles, CA, October 21, 2013; Confidential interview by Andrew Kretz, London, ON, January 30, 2014; Confidential interview by Andrew Kretz, Ottawa, ON, February 6, 2014.
127   "About ASU," *Arizona State University*, accessed November 1, 2014, http://about.asu.edu/facts.html.
128   Michael M. Crow, *A New American University Reader: Selected Writings on University Design and Related Topics* (Arizona State University: July 2011), accessed on November 1, 2014, http://president.asu.edu/sites/default/files/New%20American%20University%20Reader%20072611%20(2).pdf.
129   Karen Leland, "ASU Technopolis Elicits Strong Response, Participation," *Arizona State University*, December 17, 2003, accessed November 5, 2014, http://www.asu.edu/news/research/technopolis_121703.htm.
130   Confidential interview by Andrew Kretz, Tempe, AZ, October 31, 2013.
131   "Edson Initiative Funds Student Business Efforts," *Arizona State University*, January 27, 2006, accessed November 5, 2014, http://www.asu.edu/news/stories/200601/20060127_EDSON.htm.
132   Formed in 2003 as a wholly owned subsidiary of the Arizona State University Foundation. AzTE is contracted by ASU to manage its technology venturing, and to work with university inventors and industry to transform scientific progress into products and services. AzTE transfers technologies invented at ASU, Northern Arizona University and their affiliated research centers to the private sector by mining university research, prosecuting patents, marketing inventions, and negotiating licenses.
133   *A Permanent Revolution* (Entrepreneurship & Innovation Group, Arizona State University, 2013), accessed October 30, 2013, https://entrepreneurship.asu.edu/sites/default/files/files/Entrepreneurship-Innovation-at-ASU-2013.pdf.
134   "ASU Wins Grant to Support Women Entrepreneurs," *ASU News*, September 5, 2014, accessed November 4, 2014, https://asunews.asu.edu/20140905-womens-entrepreneurship-initiative.
135   *Changemaker Central @ ASU*, accessed November 1, 2014, http://changemaker.asu.edu/index.php.
136   "Signature Programs," *Changemaker Central@ASU*, accessed November 1, 2014, http://changemaker.asu.edu/about.php#2.
137   "Techshop," *ASU Entrepreneurship and Innovation*, accessed December 1, 2014, http://entrepreneurship.asu.edu/techshop.

## Entrepreneurship Learning on Campus 125

138 *Arizona State University* (Kansas City, MO: Ewing Marion Kauffman Foundation, 2013), accessed October 1, 2013 (http://www.kauffman.org/~/media/kauffman_org/research%20reports%20and%20covers/2013/08/kci_asu.pdf.

139 "ASU Academic Catalog," *Arizona State University*, accessed November 1, 2014, https://catalog.asu.edu/catalog_archives.

140 The development and implementation of the minor was supported by a grant from the US Department of Education's Fund for the Improvement of Postsecondary. See "Transforming the American Workforce via Entrepreneurship and Small Business Curriculum Reform," *Department of Education FIPSE Database*, accessed December 1, 2014, http://fipsedatabase.ed.gov/fipse/grantshow.cfm?grantNumber=P116B960299; Lindsey Collom, ASU Coaches Entrepreneurs from Students to Small Businesses," *The Business Journal*, August 13, 2000, accessed October 9, 2014, http://www.bizjournals.com/phoenix/stories/2000/08/14/focus1.html?page=all.

141 "Pave," *Herberger Institute for Design and the Arts, School of Film, Dance, and Theatre, Arizona State University*, accessed November 1, 2014, https://filmdancetheatre.asu.edu/initiatives/pave.

142 "Cronkite New Media Innovation and Entrepreneurship Lab," *Walter Cronkite School of Journalism and Mass Communication, Arizona State University*, accessed December 1, 2014, http://nmil.jmc.asu.edu; "ASU Launches Innovation Lab for New Media," *Walter Cronkite School of Journalism and Mass Communication, Arizona State University*, September 25, 2006, accessed September 6, 2013, https://cronkite.asu.edu/news/newMediaLab-092506; http://nmil.jmc.asu.edu.

143 Faith Miller, "Cronkite School Opens New Media Innovation Lab to Public for Business and Tech Advice," *Downtown Devil*, September 25, 2014, accessed November 24, 2014, http://downtowndevil.com/2014/09/25/61170/phoenix-cronkite-media-innovation-public/.

144 "Startup Village," Ira A. Fulton Schools of Engineering, Arizona State University, accessed November 20, 2014, http://innovation.asu.edu/startupvillage.

145 Michael M. Crow, "Reviving Our Economy: Supporting a 21st Century Workforce," *Hearing fore the Committee on Education and the Workforce, United States House of Representatives*, March 20, 2014, accessed November 20, 2014, http://edworkforce.house.gov/uploadedfiles/crow_testimony_final.pdf.

146 Claude W. Doucet, "A Brief History of Ryerson University" (Archives and Special Collections, Ryerson University: July 2007), accessed November19, 2014, https://library.ryerson.ca/asc/archives/ryerson-history/brief-history/.

147 Ryerson University, *Our Time to Lead: Academic Plan 2014–2019* (Office of the Provost and Vice President Academic, Ryerson University, June 2014),

accessed October 16, 2014, http://www.ryerson.ca/senate/agenda/2014/Academic_Plan_Draft_Full_June_3_14.pdf.

148  *Notes for an address by Sheldon Levy, President of Ryerson University to the Empire Club of Canada* (Ryerson University, March 5, 2009), accessed October 3, 2014, http://www.ryerson.ca/news/media/20090305_SheldonLevyAddress.pdf.

149  Kristen Heredia, "DMZ Ranked Fifth Globally and First in Canada in University Business Incubator's Global Ranking," *Digital Media Zone, Ryerson University*, June 25, 2014, accessed November 10, 2014, http://digitalmediazone.ryerson.ca/blog/digital-media-zone-ryerson-university-ranked-fifth-globally-first-canada-university-business-incubators-global-ranking/.

150  Heather Kearney, "Government of Canada Officially Designates 2011 as year of the Entrepreneur at Ryerson's Digital Media Zone," *Ryerson University*, January 26, 2011, accessed November 14, 2014, http://www.ryerson.ca/news/news/General_Public/20110126_yoe.html.

151  Lauren Clegg, "Digital Media Zone at Ryerson University Celebrates its Third Anniversary," *Digital Media Zone, Ryerson University*, May 1, 2013, accessed November 1, 2014, http://digitalmediazone.ryerson.ca/uncategorized/digital-media-zone-at-ryerson-university-celebrates-its-third-anniversary/.

152  "Universities," *Enactus*, accessed December 1, 2014, http://enactus.org/who-we-are/universities/.

153  For instance, the REI has hired work-study students to serve as Entrepreneur Ambassadors to help create and deliver events and resources across disciplines. Confidential interview by Andrew Kretz, Toronto, ON, November 5, 2013.

154  Steven A. Gedeon, "Instilling an Entrepreneurial Culture," in *University-Based Entrepreneurship Centres in Canada*, ed. Teresa V. Menzies (St. Catherines: Brock University), 119–128.

155  Dan Cantiller, "Building Our Residence Academic Programs: Highlights from the ACUHO-I Living Learning Programs Conference," *The Ryerson Student Affairs Blog*, November 5, 2013, accessed March 8, 2014, http://ryersonstudentaffairs.com/building-our-residence-academic-programs-highlights-from-the-acuho-i-living-learning-programs-conference/.

156  Ian Crookshank, "Residence Innovation Challenge," *The Ryerson Student Affairs Blog*, May 16, 2013, accessed October 14, 2014, http://ryersonstudentaffairs.com/residence-innovation-challenge/.

157  Ryerson University, *Our Time to Lead: Academic Plan 2014–2019* (Office of the Provost and Vice President Academic, Ryerson University, June 2014), Accessed October 16, 2014, http://www.ryerson.ca/senate/

agenda/2014/Academic_Plan_Draft_Full_June_3_14.pdf; Strategic Government of Ontario, *Mandate Agreement (2014–2017) Between the Ministry of Training, Colleges and Universities & Ryerson University*, accessed December 5, 2014, http://www.tcu.gov.on.ca/pepg/publications/vision/RyersonAgreement.pdf.

158 *Zone Learning*, Ryerson University, accessed December 20, 2014, http://www.ryerson.ca/zonelearning/.

159 Katie McDowell, "USC On Track to Raise $6 Billion by 2018," *Daily Trojan*, September 16, accessed October 8, 2014, http://dailytrojan.com/2014/09/16/usc-on-track-to-raise-6-billion-by-2018/.

160 Kathleen Allen and Mark Lieberman, "University of Southern California," in *The Development of University-Based Entrepreneurship Ecosystems*, eds. Michael L. Fetters, Patricia G. Greene, Mark P. Rice, and John Sibley Butler (Cheltenham, UK: Edward Elgar Publishing, 2010): 76–95; Katz, "The Chronology and Intellectual Trajectory of American Entrepreneurship Education: 1876–1999."

161 Confidential interview by Andrew Kretz, Los Angeles, CA, October 21, 2013; Allen and Lieberman, "University of Southern California."

162 Diane Lundin, "Alumnus Lloyd Greif's $5 Million Gift Establishes Center at the Marshall School, *USC News*, March 23, 1998, accessed October 21, 2014, https://news.usc.edu/10601/Alumnus-Lloyd-Greif-s-5-Million-Gift-Establishes-Center-at-the-Marshall-School/.

163 Allen and Lieberman, "University of Southern California."

164 "Venture Capitalist Gives $22 Million to USC Engineering School," *Philanthropy News Digest*, November 12, 2004, accessed November 12, 2014, http://philanthropynewsdigest.org/news/venture-capitalist-gives-22-million-to-usc-engineering-school.

165 Rebecca Buckman, "More Universities Support for Campus Start-Ups," *The Wall Street Journal*, November 27, 2008, accessed November 17, 2014, http://online.wsj.com/articles/SB116459586525233246.

166 Agnie Green, "USC Innovation Institute Reinventing Itself," *The Los Angeles Times*, March 29, 2007, accessed November 11, 2013, http://articles.latimes.com/2007/mar/29/local/me-innovate29.

167 "USC Appoints New Executive Director for USC Stevens Center for Innovation," PR *Newswire*, March 18, 2013, accessed November 20, 2013, http://www.prnewswire.com/news-releases/usc-appoints-new-executive-director-for-usc-stevens-center-for-innovation-198819951.html.

168 Confidential interview by Andrew Kretz, Toronto, ON, October 7, 2013.

169 "About Entrepreneurial Studies at Marshal," *Lloyd Greif Center for Entrepreneurial Studies, Marshal School of Business, University of Southern California*, accessed December 1, 2014, http://www.marshall.usc.edu/faculty/centers/greif.

170 "Teaching How to Give Back: USC Marshall Launches Soeity and Business Lab (SBL)," *News at Marshall*, September 24, 2008, accessed October 25, 2014, http://www.marshall.usc.edu/news/releases/2008/teaching-how-give-back-usc-marshall-launches-society-and-business-lab-sbl.

171 Paromita Pain, "Schools Add Minors with Global Focus," *Daily Trojan*, August 28, 2011, accessed October 15, 2014, http://dailytrojan.com/2011/08/28/schools-add-minors-with-global-focus/#sthash.vJAtOpXl.dpuf.

172 "Multi-Million Dollar Gift to Help Address Global Social Challenges," *News at Marshall*, January 21, 2014, http://www.marshall.usc.edu/news/releases/2014/multi-million-dollar-gift-help-address-global-social-challenges.

173 Mark Glaser, "USC Annenberg Pushes Innovation Lab, Experimental School, 1+Year Master's," *MediaShift*, January 18, 2013, accessed November 16, 2014, http://www.pbs.org/mediashift/2013/01/usc-annenberg-pushes-innovation-lab-experimental-school-1-year-masters018/.

174 Gretchen Parker, "USC Annenberg Announces Launch of Annenberg Innovation Lab," *USC Annenberg News*, November 17, 2010, accessed October 31, 2014, http://annenberg.usc.edu/News%20and%20Events/News/101117AIL.aspx.

175 "Blackstone LaunchPad USC," *USC Annenberg Innovation Lab*, accessed December 1, 2014, http://www.annenberglab.com/projects/blackstone-launchpadusc.

176 "Massiah Foundation, USC Viterbi School of Engineering Announce $1 Million Endowment of Maseeh Entrepreneurship Prize at Grand Challenges Summit," *USC Viterbi School of Engineering*, October 7, 2010, accessed November 3, 2014, http://viterbi.usc.edu/news/news/2010/massiah-foundation-usc.htm.

177 "Professor Peter Beerel is Appointed as Faculty Director of Innovation and Entrepreneurship in Engineering," *USC Viterbi School of Engineering*, October 22, 2010, accessed November 9, 2014, http://ceng.usc.edu/news/news/professor-peter-beerel.htm.

178 Noah Zucker, "Tech Accelerator to Grow Student Companies," *Daily Trojan*, March 31, 2013, accessed October 6, 2014, http://dailytrojan.com/2013/03/31/tech-accelerator-to-grow-student-companies/#sthash.EZNAdsdk.dpuf.

179 Cassie Paton, "NSF Funding Startups," *USC Viterbi School of* Engineering, August 8, 2014, http://viterbi.usc.edu/news/news/2014/nsf-funding-startups-usc-i-corps-site-program.htm; "Diploma in Innovation," *University of Southern California*, accessed November 20, 2014, http://idiploma.usc.edu.

180 Dan Lacovara, "Jimmy Lovine and Dr. Dre give $ 70 Million to Create New Academy at USC," *USC News*, May 15, 2013, accessed November 29, 2014, http://news.usc.edu/50816/jimmy-iovine-and-dr-dre-give-70-million-to-create-new-academy-at-usc/.

181 "USC Jimmy Lovine and Andre Young Academy," *University of Southern California*, accessed December 20, 2014, http://iovine-young.usc.edu/#home_program.

182 Jonathan Potter and Gabriela Miranda, eds., *Clusters, Innovation and Entrepreneurship* (Paris: OECD, 2009).

183 *Mid-Cycle Review Final Report* (University of Waterloo, Institutional Analysis and Planning, February 2013), accessed October 23, 2014, https://uwaterloo.ca/strategic-plan/sites/ca.strategic-plan/files/uploads/files/Mid%20Cycle%20Review%20Final%20Report_07Feb2013_0.pdf

184 Allison Bramwell and David A. Wolfe, "Universities and Regional Economic Development: The Entrepreneurial University of Waterloo," *Research Policy* 37, no. 8 (2008): 1175–1187.

185 Sean Silcoff, Jacquie McNish, and Steve Ladurantaye, "Inside the Fall of BlackBerry: How the Smartphone Inventor Failed to Adapt," *The Globe and Mail*, last updated November 6, 2013, http://www.theglobeandmail.com/report-on-business/the-inside-story-of-why-blackberry-is-failing/article14563602/?page=all.

186 David A. Wolfe, *21st Century Cities in Canada: The Geography of Innovation* (Ottawa, ON: The Conference Board of Canada, 2009).

187 Jen Nelles, Alison Bramwell, and David A. Wolfe, "History, Culture and Path Dependency: Origins of the Waterloo ICT Cluster," in *Global Networks and Local Linkages*, eds. David A. Wolfe and M. Lucas (Montreal, QC: McGill-Queen's University Press, 2005), 227–249.

188 "About Cooperative Education," *University of Waterloo*, accessed November 20, 2014, https://uwaterloo.ca/co-operative-education/about-co-operative-education.

189 Wolfe, *21st Century Cities in Canada: The Geography of Innovation*.

190 Ibid.

191 "Entrepreneurs in the Classroom: MBET Spells Success," *The Record* (advertisement by the Conrad Centre for Business, Entrepreneurship, and Technology, University of Waterloo), accessed November 1, 2014, https://uwaterloo.ca/conrad-business-entrepreneurship-technology/sites/ca.conrad-business-entrepreneurship-technology/files/uploads/files/controller_0.pdf.

192 "UW Innovate Inc. Officially Opens for Business," *@uWaterloo*, September 2002, accessed November 6, 2014, http://alumni.uwaterloo.ca/alumni/e-newsletter/2002/sept/innovate_inc_officially_opens.htm; "More Money for Innovate Inc.," *Daily Bulletin*, April 26, 2002, http://www.bulletin.uwaterloo.ca/2002/apr/26fr.html.

193 "Not Just Business, It's BET," *Daily Bulletin*, March 25, 2002, accessed October 14, 2014, http://www.bulletin.uwaterloo.ca/2002/mar/25mo.html; "'We Need a Business Presence,'" *Daily Bulletin*, May 28, 1999, accessed October 30, 2014, http://www.bulletin.uwaterloo.ca/1999/may/28fr.html.

194 "Senate Sees New Innovation Draft," *Daily Bulletin*, December 16, 2002, accessed October 3, 2014, http://www.bulletin.uwaterloo.ca/2002/dec/16mo.html.

195 Adel S. Sedra, *Vision 2010: First Annual Progress Report on the Faculty of Engineering's Strategic Plan* (Faculty of Engineering, University of Waterloo, May 2007), accessed November 6, 2014, https://uwaterloo.ca/engineering/sites/ca.engineering/files/uploads/files/vision2010_PlanUpdate2007.pdf.

196 Adel S. Sedra, *Vision 2010: Second Annual Progress Report on the Faculty of Engineering's Strategic Plan* (Faculty of Engineering, University of Waterloo, May 2008), accessed November 6, 2014, https://uwaterloo.ca/engineering/sites/ca.engineering/files/uploads/files/Vision2010_PlanUpdate2008.pdf.

197 "University President Appoints Dr. Howard Armitage Special Advisor, Entrepreneurship," *Press release of the Conrad Business, Entrepreneurship and Technology Centre, University of Waterloo*, June 28, 2013, accessed March 6, 2014, https://uwaterloo.ca/conrad-business-entrepreneurship-technology/sites/ca.conrad-business-entrepreneurship-technology/files/uploads/files/Howard%20Appoitment%202013%20%28final%29.pdf.

198 Léo Charbonneau, "Waterloo's Incubator Residence," *University Affairs*, April 7, 2008, accessed November 16, 2014, http://www.universityaffairs.ca/news/news-article/waterloos-incubator-residence/.

199 "Waterloo's VeloCity: Creating the Next-Generation of Entrepreneurs," Ontario Business Report, July, 2012, accessed November 12, 2014, http://www.mri.gov.on.ca/obr/2012/07/waterloos-velocity-creating-the-next-generation-of-entrepreneurs/#sthash.QoXCFULc.dpuf.

200 "23-Year-Old Donates US$1-Million to Support University of Waterloo Student Entrepreneurs," *VeloCity, University of Waterloo*, March 29, 2011, accessed November 14, 2014, http://velocity.uwaterloo.ca/2011/03/23-year-old-donates-us1-million-to-support-university-of-waterloo-student-entrepreneurs/.

201 "Velocity Fund," *VeloCity, University of Waterloo*, accessed November 5, 2014, http://velocity.uwaterloo.ca/velocity-fund/.

202 "Stratford Accelerator Centre to Join University of Waterloo Stratford Campus," *Accelerator Centre*, February 21, 2014, accessed October 20, 2014, http://acceleratorcentre.com/2014/02/stratford-accelerator-centre-to-join-university-of-waterloo-stratford-campus/.

203 *Vision 2015: Building on Excellence, Waterloo Engineering Strategic Plan Progress Report 2012/2013* (Office of the Dean of Engineering, Faculty of Engineering, University of Waterloo, November, 2013), accessed November 14, 2014, https://uwaterloo.ca/engineering/sites/ca.engineering/files/uploads/files/vision_2015_progress_report_2013_final_0.pdf.

204 University of Waterloo, *University of Waterloo Proposals for Major Capacity Expansion Program*, June 27, 2014, accessed November 5, 2014, http://www.tcu.gov.on.ca/pepg/publications/vision/notices/waterlooEngineering.pdf.

205 Restrictions to the maturation and legitimation of entrepreneurship education are said to include the marginalization of entrepreneurship teaching and research by business schools, and within the business management field in general [Donald F. Kuratko, "The Emergence of Entrepreneurship Education: Development, Trends, and Challenges," *Entrepreneurship Theory and Practice* 29, no. 5 (2005): 577–598; Mike Wright, Evila Piva, Simon Mosey, and Andy Lockett, "Academic Entrepreneurship and Business Schools," *The Journal of Technology Transfer* 34, no. 6 (2009): 560–587], in addition to the short supply of faculty knowledgeable and experienced in entrepreneurship [Kuratko, "The Emergence of Entrepreneurship Education: Development, Trends, and Challenges"; Robert P. Singh, "The Shortage of Academically Trained Entrepreneurship Faculty: Implications, Challenges, and Opportunities," *Journal of Entrepreneurship Education* 11 (2008): 117–131], sporadic administrative support attributable to a limited number of institutional stakeholders and champions of entrepreneurship education [Kuratko, "The Emergence of Entrepreneurship Education: Development, Trends, and Challenges"; Katz, "Fully Mature but Not Fully Legitimate: A Different Perspective on the State of Entrepreneurship Education"; Menzies, *Entrepreneurship and the Canadian Universities: Strategies and Best Practices of Entrepreneurship Centres*], and lack of funding [ibid.].

206 Cooper H. Langford, Peter Josty, and J. Adam Holbrook, *Global Entrepreneurship Monitor: Canada National Report* (London, UK: Global Entrepreneurship Monitor, 2013); Donna J. Kelley, Abdul Ali, Canadida Brush, Andrew Corbett, Mahdi Majbouri, and Edward Rogoff, *Global Entrepreneurship Monitor: United States National Report* (London, UK: Global Entrepreneurship Monitor, 2013).

# 5
# Conclusions

**Abstract:** *This concluding chapter reflects on the entrepreneurship movement and its impact on higher education. The institutional basis supporting the growth of entrepreneurship education at colleges and universities are underscored. As entrepreneurial learning and practice take hold in universities, multiple participants in the entrepreneurship movement are drawn to campus. This has brought higher education institutions in closer cooperation with a range of external communities into multiple kinds of relationships. The chapter ends with an argument for why the entrepreneurship movement is likely to remain relevant to higher education for the foreseeable future.*

Sá, Creso M. and Andrew J. Kretz. *The Entrepreneurship Movement and the University.* New York: Palgrave Macmillan, 2015. DOI: 10.1057/9781137401014.0008.

This book started by sketching out the social, economic, technological, and policy trends that have propelled entrepreneurship in higher education. Broad social and political support for entrepreneurship has created heightened and arguably unrealistic expectations around the overall contribution of entrepreneurs to the economy. Entrepreneurship scholar Scott Shane has argued that expectations behind the general support to entrepreneurs in the United States amount to an "illusion." That is, the odds of success for the average entrepreneur, as well as the likelihood that the average start-up company will significantly contribute to economic activity, are low. Shane sees policymakers, investors, and entrepreneurs themselves as influenced by the very rare cases of start-up companies that beat the odds and achieve spectacular success. Those exceptions, he argues, do not warrant the faith posed on maximizing entrepreneurial activity across sectors, and turning large numbers of individuals into new business owners.[1]

Even as he delivers these cautionary warnings about efforts to induce entrepreneurship, Shane argues that attention and resources should be concentrated on the small subset of entrepreneurs and start-ups that can make the most meaningful contributions to innovation and economic activity: the ones bringing together highly educated individuals with well-devised business ideas. These are the knowledge-intensive companies in growing technological sectors of the economy. New companies of this sort are expected to generate breakthroughs and create the most economic value. This small subset of high-tech start-ups is exactly the target of public policies involving universities in entrepreneurial activity, and the prized outcome that academic leaders seek from their campuses' entrepreneurship education initiatives.

The ethos of entrepreneurship has pervaded higher education largely since the 1980s—although to be sure, some universities have an even longer tradition welcoming and nurturing the entrepreneurial engagements of their faculty and students. Entrepreneurship at universities has traditionally been confined to patenting and licensing the results of faculty research, and to a more limited extent generating companies founded on university-based research.[2] However, the activities and expectations associated with technology transfer activities have helped to normalize the dissemination of entrepreneurship education across college and university campuses. Yet, entrepreneurship education is not driven entirely by financial or market incentives. Rather, it is the result of a pervasive social, cultural, and political movement backed by various stakeholders. The proliferation of academic programs, experiential learning opportunities, idea pads, accelerators, affinity groups, student clubs, and living-learning communities results from the broad base of support for and interest in entrepreneurship. Viewed broadly, all these offerings flourishing in higher education are manifestations of what we have termed the entrepreneurship movement. They represent efforts to impart the knowledge, skills, values, and attitudes associated with entrepreneurship, which may or may not be directly related to the expectation of launching new companies.

We have discussed in the previous chapters the overall scale of entrepreneurial activity in Canada and the United States, the evolving policy landscape promoting high-tech venture creation, and the organizational models of entrepreneurship learning employed in universities. In doing so, we have not taken on a normative perspective as to whether universities *should* participate in efforts to educate entrepreneurs or spur start-ups. The involvement of universities with the logics of the marketplace has long been a contentious issue. In our view, the developments we identified and analyzed are neither intrinsically desirable nor unavoidably destined to corrupt higher education institutions. Such valuations need to be context-specific. As clear from the previous chapters, entrepreneurial initiatives in universities are highly decentralized, and involve diverse sets of communities placed on and off campus and with variegated goals. At major universities, it is virtually impossible to offer a generic account of what is happening with entrepreneurship on campus that does justice to the multiple programs and organizations involved. As such, positive and negative outcomes of university entrepreneurial initiatives need to be qualified by the nature of the underlying activity.

As we near the mid-2010s, entrepreneurship-related offerings in universities seem to be diversifying into an increasing number of organizational models and programmatic activities. From the classroom to incubators to student housing, entrepreneurship has been taken up on campuses as a motif worth pursuing. If anything, this trend seems to be growing stronger. It is anchored in the consolidation of the entrepreneurship field of study, the wide appropriation of the concept across academic disciplines, and in the backing of academic leaders who build and promote campus programs. These are the institutional basis of the entrepreneurship movement in academia, which supports the proliferation of centers, programs, and other offerings.

## The institutional basis of the entrepreneurship movement in universities

One key element that helps academic subjects gain respectability in higher education is the establishment of an academic research base. Inside universities, the academic field of entrepreneurship studies has become consolidated since its emergence in the late 1970s. Universities' educational offerings find a theoretical base in the research field, which has become increasingly institutionalized. An assessment of the field indicates that "publication opportunities have increased dramatically," "new mechanisms have emerged that recognize and reward individual scholarship," and that research "training and mentoring has moved from the old apprenticeship system to a much more collective model."[3] The support from foundations discussed in previous chapters has also been instrumental in changing "the scale and scope of entrepreneurship research."[4] An established and growing research field, with specialized scholars whose main professional identity is tied to entrepreneurship, is a critical foundation for the continued growth of entrepreneurial studies. A research base and close links to the entrepreneurial community helps shape a distinctive orientation for entrepreneurship education that sets it apart from general management education.[5]

While there are some academic departments and schools in the field, entrepreneurship centers are still common institutional homes for the field on university campuses. These organizational units are not new on university campuses, but they are moving away from exclusively catering to business students and becoming increasingly focused on the integration of programs and activities aimed at fostering student entrepreneurship and venture creation across disciplines. The wide variety of activities they undertake denote their important role in coordinating academic and extracurricular offerings.[6] Most centers are located within business schools although a growing number are becoming established within engineering schools as well as the arts. Others are independent units serving campus-wide entrepreneurship education for students across disciplines.[7]

Previous chapters have shown that multiple trends have compelled the greater involvement of universities in supporting student entrepreneurship. Many other academic fields of study have evolved in recent decades, without necessarily drawing on the campus-wide attention that entrepreneurship does.[8] The popularity of the concept in higher education clearly outgrows the field of entrepreneurship per se. As Chapter 4 demonstrates, entrepreneurial thinking and practice have spread within universities across fields of study during the last two decades. Schools of engineering, science, social science, and professional fields organize academic programs, courses, workshops, accelerators, mentorship programs, among other offerings in entrepreneurship. The ideas and values entrepreneurship represents, such as innovation, leadership, self-reliance, creativity, problem-solving, and social change, are embraced by new and long-standing academic disciplines alike. As we have shown, much of the recent growth of entrepreneurship courses and programs are intended for nonbusiness majors. Parallels have been traced between entrepreneurship and the liberal arts (Chapter 4). These efforts to overlay liberal arts education with the skills of an entrepreneur may be viewed as attempts to enhance the relevance of a liberal arts education. At the same time, they demonstrate the familiarity and diffusion of entrepreneurship learning in the academy.

Moreover, this expansion resonates with the preferences of students. The popularity of entrepreneurship among students provides universities with a strong motivation to support entrepreneurial learning. In the United States, roughly 43 percent of incoming freshman report that becoming successful in a business of their own is essential or very important,[9] and several studies have demonstrated that students from diverse disciplinary backgrounds are interested in learning about entrepreneurship.[10] Considering the interests of the college-going cohort, several news sources have recently begun ranking university and college entrepreneurship programs.[11] Although numerous scholars have raised concerns about the validity and importance of rankings, students and academic leaders use them to make decisions—the perceived benefits of being associated with a successful university or program may attract students, donor income, and industry funding.[12] In this context, higher education leaders tend to find it in their interest to adapt to the entrepreneurial interests of today's students. Adapting the idea of entrepreneurship to new disciplines unrelated from business can be a source of increased student enrollments.[13]

Furthermore, entrepreneurship has gained legitimacy on campuses in part through public expectations of the economic and social relevance of higher education. Many leaders of higher education institutions have aligned themselves with public priorities and have positioned their institutions to support entrepreneurship education. In one collective demonstration of support for the cause, academic leaders at 142 universities endorsed recommendations generated by the American Association of Universities (AAU) and the Association of Public Land Grant Universities (APLU), for how government, universities, and the private sector could partner to advance university-based innovation and entrepreneurship. Similar efforts to foster entrepreneurship have been pursued by the National Association of Community College Entrepreneurship (NACCE) and the Historically Black Colleges and Universities (HBCU) community, through the work of the United Negro College Fund and the HBCU Business School Deans.[14] In Canada, the Council of Ontario Universities, representing the country's largest university system, similarly endorsed the provision of entrepreneurial learning and practice across the province's campuses.[15]

Universities have also created senior-level administrative positions to champion entrepreneurship and oversee related initiatives. Some universities have added that responsibility to the role of vice presidents for research, while others have created entirely new positions, such as vice president and university dean for entrepreneurship & innovation (Arizona State University), associate vice chancellor for entrepreneurship (University of California at Los Angeles), special advisor to the president for entrepreneurship (University of Waterloo), and executive director for entrepreneurship within the VP research office (University of Ottawa). Universities assign such roles typically in efforts to coordinate entrepreneurship education on campus and make courses and programs visible and accessible to all students across disciplines.[16] These roles also have an important symbolic role, as they demonstrate publicly that entrepreneurship has a voice in the university leadership.

## Advocates, evangelizers, and change agents

As entrepreneurial learning and practice take hold in universities, multiple participants in the entrepreneurship movement are drawn to campus. University initiatives in the field are often integrated with external communities of varying responsibilities in promoting entrepreneurship. Such external communities include nonprofit organizations evangelizing the virtues of entrepreneurship, philanthropists dedicated to building the field, proponent of business models of entrepreneurship, public agencies providing services to entrepreneurs, and agents involved in supporting, capitalizing, and transacting with start-up companies. This has brought higher education institutions in closer cooperation with a range of external communities into multiple kinds of relationships.

Entrepreneurship is a shared field of academic research, learning, and practice that creates a common space for individuals conventionally separated by traditional institutional boundaries in academia. The teaching of entrepreneurship spans departments and disciplines, and now commonly involves unconventional settings such as "ideapads," "garages," and "hatcheries," as seen in Chapter 4. Even if the specific focus and objective of entrepreneurship education differs across programs, common mindsets, skills, and strategies provide a shared learning context. Students from multiple disciplines often enroll in the same entrepreneurship course and participate together in entrepreneurship activities on campus. External communities play an important role in the setup and operation of entrepreneurship programs and activities on campus, not only supporting the provision of curricular and extracurricular opportunities but also participating in their delivery. Entrepreneurs, alumni, and government and nongovernment organizations are some of the external actors who participate in mentoring, advising, funding, and endorsing entrepreneurship programs on campuses.

Previous chapters have demonstrated that philanthropists are significant sponsors of university entrepreneurship centers and endowed professorships.[17] The Coleman Foundation is one such benefactor in the United States, having established chairs and professorships in colleges and universities. Similarly, the John Dobson Foundation promotes entrepreneurial activities and education in Canadian universities.[18] Foundations have also supported the curricular integration of entrepreneurship into general undergraduate education, quite prominently in the case of the Kauffman Foundation in the United States. The Coleman Foundation too has contributed to the diffusion of entrepreneurship outside the school of business by sponsoring faculty who teach in other disciplines.[19] Endowed centers and professor positions are vehicles through which entrepreneurial thinking has found an academic home on campuses.

"Boundary spanners"—individuals or organizations that operate across fundamentally different organizations or sectors of society[20]—are key actors in the diffusion of entrepreneurship in higher education. The endorsement of entrepreneurship education by academic leaders, the financial support of individuals and groups external to higher education institutions, and the expectations from governments and students have provided powerful incentives for universities to embrace entrepreneurship. While this has helped increase the acceptance of entrepreneurship in higher education, boundary spanners facilitate the development of campus entrepreneurial initiatives and communities. They bring ideas, practices, organizational models, expertise, and other resources related to entrepreneurship into the university. They also navigate academic norms and university organizational structures to adjust and blend entrepreneurial offerings into the university context. Overall, boundary spanners connect institutions with surrounding entrepreneurial communities, contributing to a two-way flow of ideas, information, and resources.

A notable type of boundary spanner is the seasoned entrepreneur who plays various roles in the operation of entrepreneurship programs. Many programs benefit from clinical faculty, such as an entrepreneur-in-residence, who are experienced entrepreneurs paid by the university to mentor and coach students with entrepreneurial aspirations. These entrepreneurs supplement the work of academic staff by teaching courses, facilitating workshops, and advising programs while operating their own start-ups and established businesses. Their job is also to help guide the flow of innovation across departments by connecting researchers and students on campus with each other and with external actors.[21] Furthermore, entrepreneurship programs generally require the support of volunteers from local entrepreneur/business communities. Apart from mentoring students in all aspects of a new venture, these community entrepreneurs also provide guest lectures, judge competitions, host student interns, serve as board members on student start-ups, and evaluate programs.[22] Volunteers also serve on advisory boards established by entrepreneurship centers and programs. These boards reflect the integration of practice and research, and are comprised of advocates for entrepreneurship, representing industry, business, finance, and the not-for-profit sector. Board members provide strategic and tactical support, raise funds, use personal networks to increase collaboration across contexts, and help bolster a program's reputation.

Another type of boundary spanner is business professionals with entrepreneurial experience, who may be hired as directors of entrepreneurship centers or head on-campus incubators. In addition to bringing their experience and networks, these entrepreneurs tend to operate in entrepreneurial centers as if they are part of a start-up.[23] They cultivate a brand by hiring marketing and communications staff to write press releases and maintain a visible web presence, and bootstrap existing resources while seeking external funding.[24] In this way, entrepreneurship centers are embedded within the start-up culture of entrepreneurship communities, and internalize that culture on campus.

Some centers coordinate and receive support from their institutions' Technology Transfer Office (TTO), which are also boundary-spanning units. TTOs generally have experience in starting new enterprises from university technology. Nonetheless, as managers of university intellectual property, TTOs may not always be well positioned to fulfill this role. It is usual for TTOs to be run on a cost-recovery basis, under the assumption that licensing revenues will generate enough funding to maintain their operation. That is however hardly the case, as most TTOs struggle to break even. As such, they may shy away from working with start-up companies with limited resources to afford upfront licensing fees, and whose future prospects are uncertain.[25] Nonetheless, as discussed in Chapter 4, an array of organizational models has flourished on campuses with an exclusive focus on start-ups. These boundary-spanning units include accelerators and hatcheries, which coexist with the older technology parks and innovation centers. These relatively new units often tap the existing internal and external expertise provided by TTOs for management guidance, technical assistance and consulting, dedicated workspace, access to shared business services, technology support services, and assistance in securing funding.

These models of entrepreneurship education internalize practices and methodologies from the entrepreneurship community. Campus-based accelerators for instance adopt many of the core elements of community-based private accelerators: an open, highly competitive application process; pre-seed investments for admitted ventures; run as a cohort model focused on small teams, not individual founders; time-limited support comprising clear goal of funding or growth and periodic assessments or milestones.[26] They often culminate in an event called Demo Day, which involves each start-up in the cohort presenting their venture to an audience of potential investors, media, sponsors, partners, alumni, and others.[27] Although typically located on campus, both incubators and accelerators operate through a network of individuals and organizations that extend beyond the university or college to include community entrepreneurs, industry contacts, venture capitalists, and angel investors.[28] It is precisely this close relationship across the academic and business worlds that make these types of programs relevant to participants.

Entrepreneurship education brings together various actors and organizations into a common field with shared ideas, ideologies, and practices. It extends across college departments through academic programs and support units, forming a context familiar to both academic and entrepreneurial communities. Both academic staff and communities outside of universities guide educational processes and outcomes. Boundary spanners maintain this shared field through the constant borrowing, translation, and adaption of practices and ideas. They are also responsible for the growing entrepreneurial ecosystem on campuses that includes incubators, workshops, pitch competitions, and start-up events. They serve as teachers, mentors, advisors, and evaluators, bringing in ideas and practices of the entrepreneurship realm into academia. They also connect institutions of higher education with surrounding entrepreneurial communities.

## Directions for the entrepreneurship movement

The entrepreneurship movement shows no sign of abating in the near future. There are multiple reasons for this, which relate the idea that entrepreneurship can and should be encouraged and supported. First, entrepreneurial offerings on campus aim at achieving a broad set of goals that are not dependent on actual start-up activity. As the previous chapter has shown, university entrepreneurship programs have variegated goals and orientations. While the growth of start-ups are obviously the raison d'être of accelerators and incubators, a whole range of curricular and extracurricular offerings are decoupled from an immediate expectation that participants will be business owners. Entrepreneurship education's growing acceptance across disciplines stems largely from the multidisciplinary applicability of entrepreneurial practice and thinking to diverse contexts and activities. For instance, proponents of infusing entrepreneurship into nonbusiness courses find value in the subject's emphasis on managing risk, spotting opportunities, and innovating, all of which are generally deemed essential skills and aptitudes favored in the contemporary economy.[29] Entrepreneurship within engineering and the arts, for example, are perceived as a way to bolster students' skills and labor market competitiveness.[30] Furthermore, liberal arts scholars have helped the acceptance of entrepreneurship outside of business schools by highlighting the parallels between a liberal arts education and the development of entrepreneurial behavior. Both teach students to approach problems in novel ways and allow them to develop a comfort with ambiguity.[31] Support for entrepreneurship education draws further strength from connections made between an entrepreneurial mindset and life-long learning—a major outcome of higher education espoused by educational institutions and governments alike—as well as from calls for more innovative and experiential educational practices.[32] The malleability in the uses of entrepreneurship in universities make the presence of the subject on campus less dependent on the success of a single academic or professional project. This allows entrepreneurial initiatives to expand regardless of the specific circumstances surrounding firm creation in universities, or the economic climate for entrepreneurial activity more broadly.

Second, engagement with start-up creation is a highly uncertain activity, and as such universities can claim credit for their efforts even if present outcomes fall short of expectations. There are several pitfalls facing would-be entrepreneurs, not the least surviving the "valley of death" represented by the scarce financing available for those with a promising invention in need of considerable development before they are market-ready.[33] Even those companies that succeed in obtaining support from investors experience a high failure rate.[34] Such is the prevalence of failure that the start-up community, or at least part of it, has come to embrace it.[35] Catchphrases such as "fail fast" have caught on as proponents normalize the usual experience of failure among entrepreneurs as an acceptable part of their journey.[36] Analysts of start-up activity provide a more complex perspective of what constitutes failure in venture creation, differentiating between firm and founder failures. The former relates to the inability to generate revenues and expected returns on investments; the latter concerns founders' losses of capital and even their positions in start-ups.[37] In this context, the efforts of universities to cultivate entrepreneurs can be expected to result in failures, without implying that programs and initiatives are necessarily ineffective. Tolerance for failure in entrepreneurial activity is hailed as a positive attribute of regions such as Silicon Valley, or the United States more generally speaking, as compared to other countries (Chapter 2). The implication for proponents and leaders of campus-based entrepreneurship programs is clear: unsuccessful outcomes in conceiving, launching, and growing a business can be disappointing, but should not doom would-be entrepreneurs, nor the larger effort to support them.

Third, the role of universities within policy efforts to promote innovation remains unchallenged, as does the role of start-ups in bringing new technologies to the marketplace. Universities gain valuable resources from public policies supporting high-tech start-ups (Chapter 3). The role of universities in policies seeking to stimulate innovation has been established over the last four decades and is now taken as a matter of course. It is well established that while firms are the key actors in generating innovation, universities are an important institution underpinning the ecosystem that supports and enables innovative activity. At the same time, the ability of academic institutions to support the creation of commercial ventures has remained unquestioned, and challenges to the wisdom of investing in university-based entrepreneurship have largely subsided, at least publicly. After some trepidation in the 1990s, US states have turned to universities with renewed vigor since around 2000 as partners in promoting technology-based economic development.[38] Canadian provinces have similarly pursued the technological and commercial fruits of world-class scientific research during the last two decades.[39] In this context, governments have been active in supporting campus-based efforts to stimulate high-tech entrepreneurs. For instance, the government of Ontario has devoted CAD$20 million to support university or college campus-based business accelerators and other on-campus entrepreneurship activities. One of the stated goals of this new funding is to build the most entrepreneurial postsecondary system in North America.[40] Since the Great Recession, renewed emphasis has been placed on stimulating start-ups (Chapter 3).

Finally, the development of vibrant start-up communities where they do not exist is knowingly a long-term proposition, which compels and justifies continuing policy and institutional efforts to planting the seed of an entrepreneurial culture. A body of research shows that initiatives to stimulate viable start-up communities need to aim at the long term.[41] Clearly, not all places will succeed in fostering a strong culture of entrepreneurship, where virtuous cycles of firm creation, growth, reinvestment, competition, and cooperation take place. Nonetheless, the wide appeal of universities contributing to this cause justifies the present efforts as steps that need to be taken toward a better future. Major hubs of entrepreneurship such as Research Triangle in North Carolina and the Waterloo region in Ontario followed decades-long cycles of development. Knowledge of those stories, encapsulated as the "lessons learned" that think tanks and foundations disseminate, provide a rationale for many higher education institutions in variegated settings to stand behind initiatives to cultivate entrepreneurialism. Notably, efforts to inculcate entrepreneurial aspirations in students might lead them to emigrate from areas where opportunities to start a firm are not as good. Still, taking an active stand on promoting entrepreneurship remains a more powerful prescription for university action, which resonates with public and private expectations.

The diffusion of entrepreneurial programming in universities represents an adaptation to social expectations for economic and social relevancy, which are embedded in the ideation of the entrepreneurship movement. The practices of academic institutions to foster student entrepreneurship and the creation of start-up companies reinforce the long-term trend of greater university engagement with economic development and closer relations with the private sector.[42] While the entrepreneurial movement intersects with the logics guiding university technology transfer, that latter is multifaceted activity that goes beyond venture creation. Moreover, university support for student entrepreneurship and the increasing penetration of the subject into the education mission denotes a much broader sphere of influence than just research in science and technology disciplines. Student demand is an important factor driving expansion of entrepreneurial education, which is fueled by the support of private donors and foundations. For the reasons laid out above, this trend is likely to persist in the near future. Universities stand to gain popularity, support, and resources from their engagement with the entrepreneurial movement. Under these circumstances, they will continue to boast the successes of their student and faculty start-ups, and to welcome programs that advance the learning and practice of entrepreneurship on their campuses.

# Notes

1  Scott Shane, *Illusions of Entrepreneurship* (New Haven, CT: Yale University Press, 2008).
2  Scott Shane, *Academic Entrepreneurship: University Spinoffs and Wealth Creation* (Cheltenham, UK: Edward Elgar Publishing, 2004); Roger L. Geiger and Creso Sá, *Tapping the Riches of Science: Universities and the Promise of Economic Growth* (Cambridge, MA: Harvard University Press: 2008).
3  Howard Aldrich, "The Emergence of Entrepreneurship as an Academic Field: A Personal Essay on Institutional Entrepreneurship," *Research Policy* 41, no. 7 (September 2012): 1242.

4   Ibid.
5   William B. Gartner and Karl H. Vesper, "Experiments in Entrepreneurship Education: Success and Failures," *Journal of Business Venturing* 9 (1994): 179–187; Jerome A. Katz, "Fully Mature But Not Fully Legitimate: A Different Perspective on the State of Entrepreneurship Education," *Journal of Small Business Management* 46, no. 4 (2008): 550–566; Donald F. Kuratko, "The Emergence of Entrepreneurship Education: Development, Trends, and Challenges," *Entrepreneurship Theory and Practice* 29, no. 5 (2005): 577–598; George T. Solomon and Lloyd. W. Fernald Jr., "Trends in Small Business Management and Entrepreneurship Education in the United States." *Entrepreneurship Theory and Practice* 15, no. 3 (1991): 25–39.
6   Todd A. Finkle, Donald F. Kuratko, and Michael G. Goldsby, "An Examination of Entrepreneurship Centers in the United States: A National Survey," *Journal of Small Business Management* 44, no. 2 (2006): 184–206; Todd A. Finkle, Teresa A. Menzies, Donald F. Kuratko, and Michael G. Goldsby, "Financial Activities of Entrepreneurship Centers in the United States," *Journal of Business and Entrepreneurship* 23, no. 2 (2012): 48–64; Teresa V. Menzies, *Entrepreneurship and the Canadian Universities: Strategies and Best Practices of Entrepreneurship Centres* (St. Catharines, ON: Faculty of Business, Brock University; John Dobson Foundation, 2000); Menzies, *Entrepreneurship and the Canadian Universities* (2009).
7   Michael H. Morris, Donald F. Kuratko, and Jeffrey R. Cornwall, *Entrepreneurship Programs and the Modern University* (Northampton, MA: Edward Elgar Publishing, 2013); Creso Sá, Andrew Kretz, and Kristjan Sigurdson, *The State of Entrepreneurship Education in Ontario's Colleges and Universities* (Higher Education Quality Council of Ontario, 2014).
8   Steve Brint, Mark Riddle, Lori Turk-Bicakci, and Charles S. Levy, "From the Liberal to the Practical Arts in American Colleges and Universities: Organizational Analysis and Curricular Change," *The Journal of Higher Education* 76, no. 2 (2005) 151–180.
9   John H. Pryor and E. J. Reedy, *Trends in Business Interest Among US College Students: An Early Exploration of Data Available From the Cooperative Institutional Research Program* (Kansas City, MO: Ewing Marion Kauffman Foundation, 2009), accessed August 5, 2014, http://papers.ssrn.com/sol3/papers.cfm?abstract_id=1971393.
10  Nancy M. Levenburg, Paul M. Lane, and Thomas V. Schwarz, "Interdisciplinary Dimensions in Entrepreneurship," *Journal of Education for Business* 81, no. 5 (2006): 275–281; Matthew J. Mayhew, Jeffrey S. Simonoff, William J. Baulmol, Batia M. Wiesenfeld, and Michael W. Klein, "Exploring Innovative Entrepreneurship and Its Ties to Higher Educational Experiences," *Research in Higher Education* 53 (2012): 831–859; Rachel Shinner, Mark Pruett, and Bryan Toney, "Entrepreneurship Education: Attitudes Across Campus," *Journal of Education for Business* 84, no. 3 (2009): 151–158.

11  For example, *US News and World Report, Entrepreneur Magazine, Success Magazine, Financial Times, Bloomberg BusinessWeek, Startup Genome,* and *UBI Index*.

12  Simon Marginson, "Dynamics of National and Global Competition in Higher Education," *Higher Education* 52, no. 1 (2006):1–39; Christopher C. Morphew and Christopher Swanson, "On the Efficacy of Raising Your University's Rankings," in *University Rankings: Theoretical Basis, Methodology, and Impacts on Global Higher Education*, eds. Jung C. Shin, Robert K. Toutkoushian, and Ulrich Teichler (Netherlands: Springer, 2011), 185–199; Ellen Hazelkorn, *Rankings and the Reshaping of Higher Education: The Battle for World-Class Excellence* (New York: Palgrave Macmillan, 2011); William Locke, "The Institution of Rankings: Managing Status Anxiety in an Increasingly Marketized Environment," in *University Rankings: Theoretical Basis, Methodology, and Impacts on Global Higher Education*, eds. Jung C. Shin, Robert K. Toutkoushian, and Ulrich Teichler (The Netherlands: Springer, 2011), 201–228.

13  Mars, for example, found through interviews with senior faculty members at one university that the inclusion of entrepreneurship into social science and liberal arts curricula was a strategy for attracting students and increasing departmental enrollments. Matthew M. Mars, "The Diverse Agendas of Faculty within an Institutionalized Model of Entrepreneurship Education," *Journal of Entrepreneurship Education* 10, no. 1 (2007): 43–62.

14  Office of Innovation and Entrepreneurship, *The Innovative and Entrepreneurial University: Higher Education, Innovation, and Entrepreneurship in Focus* (Washington, DC: US Department of Commerce, 2013), accessed March 14, 2014, http://www.eda.gov/pdf/The_Innovative_and_Entrepreneurial_University_Report.pdf.

15  Council of Ontario Universities, *Entrepreneurship at Ontario Universities: Fuelling Success* (Toronto, ON: Council of Ontario Universities, 2014).

16  In Ontario, the rise of such positions is in part reaction to new funding schemes requiring cross-campus entrepreneurship coordination.

17  Jerome Katz, *2004 Survey of Endowed Positions in Entrepreneurship and Related Fields in the United States* (2004), http://sites.kauffman.org/pdf/survey_endowed_chairs_04.pdf; Michael R. Bowers, C. M. Bowers, and Gabriel Ivan, "Academically-Based Entrepreneurship Centers: An Exploration of Structure and Function," *Journal of Entrepreneurship Education* 9 (2006): 1–14; Finkle, Menzies, Kuratko, and Goldsby, "Financial Activities of Entrepreneurship Centers in the United States."

18  "John Dobson," *Norman Newman Centre for Entrepreneurship, Dalhousie University*, accessed November 20, 2014, http://www.dal.ca/faculty/management/nnce/about/our-partners/john-dobson.html.

19  See: "Coleman Entrepreneurship Chairs & Professorships," The Coleman Foundation, accessed November 20, 2014, http://www.colemanfoundation.org/what_we_fund/entrepreneurship/entrepreneurship-chairs.html.

20  Michael L. Tushman, "Special Boundary Roles in the Innovation Process," *Administrative Science Quarterly* 22, no. 4 (1977): 587–605.
21  See early work on such role by boundary-spanners in organizations: James D. Thomson, *Organizations in Action* (New York: McGraw-Hill, 1967).
22  Morris, Kuratko, and Cornwall, *Entrepreneurship Programs and the Modern University*.
23  Ibid.
24  Indeed, in a survey of extracurricular entrepreneurship programs in the province of Ontario, universities and colleges only supplied 38 percent of program funding (Sá, Kretz, and Sigurdson, *The State of Entrepreneurship Education in Ontario's Colleges and Universities*).
25  Geiger and Sá, *Tapping the Riches of Science*.
26  Paul Miller and Kirsten Bound, *The Startup Factories: The Rise of Accelerator Programmes to Support New Technology Ventures* (NESTA, 2011), http://www.nesta.org.uk/sites/default/files/the_startup_factories_0.pdf.
27  Elizabeth Caley, *Seeding Success: Canada's Startup Accelerators*, ed. Helen Jula (MaRs Data Catalyst, 2013), http://www.marsdd.com/app/uploads/2014/04/20130619-datacatalyst-acceleratorreport.pdf.
28  Sean M. Hackett and David M. Dilts, "A Systematic Review of Business Incubation Research," *The Journal of Technology Transfer* 29, no. 1 (2004): 55–82.
29  Walter W. Powell and Kaisa Snellman, "The Knowledge Economy," *Annual Review of Sociology* 30, no. 1 (2004): 199–220; Erik Stam and Elizabeth Garnsey, "Entrepreneurship in the Knowledge Economy," in *Creating Wealth from Knowledge: Meeting the Innovation Challenge*, eds. John Bessant and Tim Venables (Cheltenham, UK: Edward Elgar Publishing, 2008), 145–176.
30  Mars, "The Diverse Agendas of Faculty within an Institutionalized Model of Entrepreneurship Education."
31  Mary Godwyn, "Can the Liberal Arts and Entrepreneurship Work Together? *Academe* 95, no. 1 (2009): 36–38; Dennis Ray, "Liberal Arts for Entrepreneurs," *Entrepreneurship Theory & Practice* 15, no. 2 (1990): 79–93; Matthew D. Regele and Heidi M. Neck, "The Entrepreneurship Education Sub-Ecosystem in the United States: Opportunities to Increase Entrepreneurial Activity," *Journal of Business & Entrepreneurship* (Winter 2012): 25–47; Kelly G. Shaver, "Reflections on a New Academic Path: Entrepreneurship in Arts and Sciences," *Peer Review* 7, no. 3 (2005): 21–23.
32  *Transforming Ontario Universities* (Toronto,ON: Council of Ontario Universities, October 2012), http://www.cou.on.ca/publications/reports/pdfs/transforming-ontario-universities----cou-submissio; Sebastian Fixson, "The Role of Experiential Learning in Developing Entrepreneurial Leaders," *Babson College*, accessed December 20, 2014, http://www.babson.edu/executive-education/thought-leadership/education/Pages/the-role-of-experiential-learning-in-developing-entrepreneurial-leaders.aspx; "Key

Competences for Lifelong Learning," *Europa.eu*, last updated, March 3, 2011, http://europa.eu/legislation_summaries/education_training_youth/lifelong_learning/c11090_en.htm.

33  Geiger and Sá, *Tapping the Riches of Science*.

34  Shikhar Ghosh, *Rethinking Entrepreneurial Failure: Stumbling Blocks or Stepping Stones*, Presented on December 15, 2011, Harvard Business School Club Hub, accessed December 20, 2014, www.clubhub.hbs.org/images.html?file_id=qoC1ffFud%2Fs%3D.

35  Some question the extent to which the embrace of failure in Silicon Valley is real or rhetorical. See Rob Asghar, "Why Silicon Valley's 'Fail Fast' Mantra Is Just Hype," *Forbes* (June 14, 2014), accessed November 10, 2014, http://www.forbes.com/sites/robasghar/2014/07/14/why-silicon-valleys-fail-fast-mantra-is-just-hype/.

36  Ryan Babineaux and John Krumboltz, *Fail Fast, Fail Often: How Losing Can Help You Win* (New York: Penguin, 2013).

37  Ghosh, *Rethinking Entrepreneurial Failure: Stumbling Blocks or Stepping Stones*.

38  Roger L. Geiger and Creso Sá, "Beyond Technology Transfer: US State a Policies to Harness University Research for Economic Development," *Minerva* 43, no. 1 (2005): 1–21.

39  Creso Sá, "Canadian Provinces and Public Policies for University Research," *Higher Education Policy* 23, no. 3 (2010): 335–357.

40  Legislative Assembly of Ontario, *Official Report of Debates* (November 18, 2014), 1213 (Hon. Reza Moridi), http://www.ontla.on.ca/web/house-proceedings/house_detail.do?locale=en&Date=2014-11-18.

41  See Maryann P. Feldman, "The Character of Innovative Places: Entrepreneurial Strategy, Economic Development and Prosperity," *Small Business Economics* 43, no. 1 (2014): 9–20; Maryann P. Feldman, Johanna Francis, and Janet Bercovitz, "Creating a Cluster While Building a Firm: Entrepreneurs and the Formation of Industrial Clusters," *Regional Studies* 39 (2005): 129–141.

42  Geiger and Sá, *Tapping the Riches of Science*; David C. Mowery, Richard Nelson, Bhaven Sampat, and Arvids Ziedonis, *Ivory Tower and Industrial Innovation: University-Industry Technology Transfer Before and After the Bayh-Dole Act in the United States* (Stanford: Stanford University Press, 2004).

# Index

Alacrity Foundation, 59
Alberta
   firm creation, 34
American Society for
   Engineering Education, 84
Arizona State University, 85, 94, 97–101
Arts Entrepreneurship, 85
Ashoka, 84
Atlantic Canada
   firm creation, 34
Atlantic Canada Opportunities Agency, 54
AUTM, 36

Babson College, 79
Ball State University, 61
Bay Area, 56
Baylor University, 79, 90
Boston, 6, 50, 52
Bradley University, 82
British Columbia, 52
   entrepreneurship policy, 58–61
Business Development Bank of Canada, 49
Business Development Bank of Canada Act, 49
Business-led Networks of Centres of Excellence, 56

California, 52
Canada, 21, 23, 25, 28, 40
Canada Accelerator and Incubator Program, 57
Centres of Excellence for Commercialization and Research, 57
Chicago, 65, 66
Coleman Foundation, 7, 84
Collegiate DECA, 82
Collegiate Entrepreneurs' Organization, 82, 92
Columbia University, 86

Delaware, 53
DeVry Education Group, 66
Digital Media Zone, 102, 104
District of Columbia, 53
Drexel University, 82, 95

Economic Development Administration, 55
Enactus, 82, 103
Enterprize Canada, 82
entrepreneurial
   activity in Canada, 34
   activity in the US and Canada, 21
   culture, 21
   intention, 22
   learning, 83
   networks, 30
   regions, 29
   university, 9
entrepreneurship
   academic, 9

entrepreneurship—*continued*
  advocates, 137–41, 84, 138
  centers, 82, 135
  courses, 78
  curriculum, 80
  education programs, 78
  failure, 26, 27, 142
  field, 10
  field of study, 80, 135
  first course, 78
  geography, 30
  idea of, 3–4
  innovation, 30
  innovative, 21
  job creation, 28
  opportunity, 24
  policy solution, 50
  popularity, 2
  propinquity, 29
  public policy, 5–6
  rates, 23
  replicative, 24, 26, 28
  resistance on campus, 85
  self-employment, 23, 28
  socio-cultural support for, 7–9
  student clubs, 82
  tacit knowledge, 30
entrepreneurship movement
  definition, 10
  nature, 141

Florida, 53
FounderDating, 92
Futurpreneur Canada, 57

Georgetown University, 96
Georgia Tech Research Institute, 95
Germany, 21
Global Consortium of Entrepreneurship Centers, 6, 83
Global Entrepreneurship Monitor, 21, 22
globalization, 5
Great Recession, 22

Harvard University, 8, 78, 79, 86

Illinois, 54
  entrepreneurship policy, 65–66
Illinois Institute of Technology, 66
Indiana
  entrepreneurship policy, 61–63
Indiana University, 61
industrial clusters, 30, 51
Industrial Research Assistance Program, 50, 57
information and communication technology (ICT), 6
Innovation Corps, 55

Joseph Schumpeter, 3

Kauffman Foundation, 3, 7, 84, 93
Kern Entrepreneurship Education Network, 83
knowledge-based economy, 4, 5

liberal arts, 86, 136
Los Angeles, 56

Maine, 53
MaRS Discovery District, 57, 64
Maryland, 53, 56
Massachusetts, 52
MIT, 9, 35, 51
Montreal, 34

National Academy of Sciences, 84
National Institutes of Health, 56
National Science Foundation, 55
Nevada, 53
New Brunswick, 34
New York, 52, 53, 56
New York University, 95
Newfoundland and Labrador, 34
Next36, 7
North Carolina State University, 85
Northeastern University, 79
Northwestern University, 66
Nova Scotia, 34, 54

OCAD University, 94
Office of Entrepreneurial Development, 50
Office of Innovation and Entrepreneurship, 55
Oklahoma State University, 82
Ontario, 34, 51, 52, 58
  entrepreneurship policy, 63–65
Oregon, 53
Oregon Health & Science University, 53
Oregon University System, 53

Prince Edward Island, 34
Princeton University, 91
public policy
  criticism, 67
  entrepreneurial, 51
  Great Recession, 54
  industrial recruitment, 51
  regional economic development, 50
Purdue University, 61

Quebéc, 52
  firm creation, 34
Queen's University, 91

Research Triangle, 51
Ryerson University, 104

San Diego State University, 88
San Francisco, 52
Sigma Nu Tau, 82
Silicon Valley, 6, 50
Small Business Act, 49
Small Business Administration, 50
Small Business Innovation Research, 56
Small Business Technology Transfer, 56
Social Entrepreneurship, 86
Stanford University, 8, 51, 86
start-up
  creation, 6
  crowdfunding, 95
  failure, 26

job creation, 28
summits, 90
survival rates, 26
university funding, 94
weekends, 90
StartUp America, 55
Startup Canada, 7, 92
Start-Up Visa Program, 58
StartupNY, 53
State University of New York, 53
Statistics Canada, 37

The Next 36, 92
Toronto, 34

United Kingdom, 21
United States, 21, 23, 25, 28, 40
United States Association for Small Business and Entrepreneurship, 83
university, 34–40
  accelerators, 93
  arts incubators, 94
  business plan competitions, 81
  entrepreneurship administrators, 137
  experiential learning, 87
  hackathons, 91
  incubators, 92
  living learning communities, 88
  rankings, 136
  rankings, 9
  start-up weekends, 91
  student entrepreneurship, 34–40
  students, 136
  study abroad, 89
University of British Columbia, 60
University of Calgary, 79, 91
University of California, Berkeley, 87, 89
University of California, Los Angeles, 79, 91
University of Chicago, 66
University of Connecticut, 90
University of Florida, 83, 89
University of Illinois, 54, 66, 89, 95
University of Maryland, College Park, 89

University of North Dakota, 82
University of Ottawa, 81
University of Pennsylvania, 79
University of Southern California, 78, 81, 91, 104–8
University of St Thomas, 82
University of Victoria, 60
University of Waterloo, 94, 95
University of Wisconsin, Madison, 85
University of Wisconsin, Whitewater, 66

Vancouver, 34

venture capital, 26
  in Canada, 52
  evidence of effectiveness, 96
  in the US, 52
VentureWell, 6, 84, 92
Vermont, 53
Virginia, 53

Waterloo University, 108–10
Waterloo-Kitchener, 51
Wichita State University, 79
Wilfred Laurier University, 89

York University, 79

GPSR Compliance
The European Union's (EU) General Product Safety Regulation (GPSR) is a set
of rules that requires consumer products to be safe and our obligations to
ensure this.

If you have any concerns about our products, you can contact us on

ProductSafety@springernature.com

In case Publisher is established outside the EU, the EU authorized
representative is:

Springer Nature Customer Service Center GmbH
Europaplatz 3
69115 Heidelberg, Germany

www.ingramcontent.com/pod-product-compliance
Lightning Source LLC
LaVergne TN
LVHW041955060526
838200LV00002B/30